The Good News of Genesis

Day by Day

Part One

Tim Sweetman

Authors notes:

In writing this summary of the book of Genesis I have prayerfully written each section in a manner that can be read one day at a time.

Reading in this way will allow the thoughts that are promoted within to have time to circulate and sink in without overloading our memory.

It has been said that, for most of us, our minds are most effective in receiving twenty minutes of teaching at any given moment.

Prolonged and concentrated spells of teaching tend to be counteractive and the information is not contained.

Having said that, by all means digest and enjoy in a manner that best suits you.

The book of Genesis is not a book to be taken lightly. There are plenty of insights and information within its pages to keep any serious scholar of scripture busy for many years.

The reader may find some of my own interpretations and explanations flippant at times and even humorous at others.

These light interventions are not intended to take away from the identity of the text in any way but perhaps to display the humanity of the characters involved in God's plan of salvation.

Preface:

The book of Genesis.

Genesis is a book of beginnings.

It is a foundational book; this is where it all began. It is the place where we get our answers from.

The book of Genesis is also a book of seeming conflict and discrepancies.

It is not a book of scientific or historic discovery although we will uncover many truths within its pages.

If we accept Genesis at its face value and read it as a book, word following word, as the translators have provided it, in our modern, and not so modern bible versions of scripture, we invariably have difficulty in relating the information within its pages with what we have been taught from archaeological, paleological, prehistoric and scientific findings.

Where there is a true disagreement, and these are extremely rare, it is possible that modern findings are either wrong or inaccurate. It is also possible that the interpretations that we have in our bibles are either wrong or inaccurate.

There is something to be said for both possibilities.

What we know for sure is that God cannot lie and that His word is true.

Therefore we need to look at the book of Genesis with an understanding that God is wanting to teach us something from what we are reading.

If we are to discover what those very important truths are, we must have an ear to hear what God is saying to us through the words that we read.

As we read with that understanding, having an open mind, we might uncover and correct historical misunderstandings and also acknowledge where recent findings both support and prove true what God is telling us within these pages.

The truth is that if the book of Genesis is not accurate we are on a slippery slope with regards to anything else in scripture that we understand to be true.

Therefore it is necessary that the truth is uncovered if we are to have a foundation upon which to stand.

With these factors in mind we will endeavour to uncover the book of Genesis.

Chapter 1.

In the beginning.

Gen. 1:1-5
In the beginning God created the heavens and the earth.
The earth was formless and empty, and darkness covered the deep waters.
And the Spirit of God was hovering over the surface of the waters.

Then God said, "Let there be light," and there was light.
And God saw that the light was good.
Then he separated the light from the darkness.

God called the light "day" and the darkness "night."

And evening passed and morning came, marking the first day.
Genesis 1:1-5 NLT

The book of Genesis opens with the words, 'In the beginning'.

This is one of the most well known phrases in the english language.

'In the beginning God'.

These are words that remind us of the fact that God is at the forefront of everything that ever was and ever will be.
God created.

The word 'created' can mean to bring forth, to begin, to design, to perform, to start a process, to build something from nothing and to build something from raw materials.

All of those aspects, and more, are incorporated in the phrase 'God created'.

'In the beginning, God created' can mean, 'from the very first nano second, God was in the process of creating'.

I am not going to go through the book of Genesis word by word. It is however crucial that we understand what we are discovering here in the opening sentences.

What is the author telling us?

When we see a flower grow and blossom in the garden we can look at the detail of it and marvel that God has created it.

He also created the seed that it grew from.

The flower hasn't simply appeared in the flower bed, there has been a process involved in its growth and blooming. Nevertheless God has created the flower.

The first ten words in the book of Genesis are: *'In the beginning God created the heavens and the earth'*.

Everything that we are aware of has been created by God.

It is verse two that clarifies what the first verse has told us.

'The earth was without form and void'.

It is believed that the author of Genesis was Moses, who wrote the book of Genesis during the desert wanderings of the children of Israel.

Moses wants us to understand what the situation was when God began the process of creation.

It is thought that Moses, led by God's Spirit, had in mind the state of the Israelite nation who were, at that time, raw materials, out of which God would bring something amazing.

Whether this is what Moses was thinking is an interesting idea and we can make some assumptions based on that hypothesis but we don't know what Moses was thinking when he wrote or whether he simply wrote what God's Spirit commanded him to.

It is likely that both of these promptings were involved.

Paul taught that all scripture is written for our benefit.

All Scripture is inspired by God and is useful to teach us what is true and to make us realize what is wrong in our lives. It corrects us when we are wrong and teaches us to do what is right.
2 Timothy 3:16 NLT

It is what God's Spirit led him to write for our benefit that matters to us.

'There was darkness over the deep and the Spirit of God hovered over the waters'.

The Spirit of God is that aspect of God that is active. He is God's personal presence.

The Hebrew word for the Spirit of God is *'Ruakh'.*

He is the invisible, powerful, energy of God.

We could write a book dedicated solely to the Spirit of God, as many others have.

We will stop at saying that the Spirit is always described as being 'of God'. They are one and the same God.

The Spirit was active in the creation. He is introduced to us here as being 'in the beginning'.

We are now given an outline of the process of the creation.

Then God said, "let there be light".

This is the first time that God speaks. What an awesome moment!

God said, "let there be light" and there was light.

When God speaks, what He has spoken must come to pass.

We read in the Gospel of John,

'In the beginning the Word already existed.

The Word was with God, and the Word was God.
He existed in the beginning with God.

God created everything through him, and nothing was created except through him.
The Word gave life to everything that was created, and his life brought light to everyone.

The light shines in the darkness, and the darkness can never extinguish it'.
John 1:1-5 NLT

John was introducing Jesus to his readers.

He described Jesus as *'the word'.*

In the first three verses of Genesis we have an introduction to God the Father, God the Spirit and God the Son.

These three are one God. They are central to all that is in existence.

And God saw that the light was good. Then he separated the light from the darkness.

The author isn't describing the sun and the moon at this point. We don't hear about those until verse sixteen, at the end of the fourth day.

If there is light, the source of the light is, as John describes in his introduction to Jesus, 'the word of God'.

Moses then describes this process as having been 'the first day'.

There is rhythm introduced to the narrative.

The phrase, *'and the evening passed and the morning came'* is repeated after each act of creation much like the chorus in a children's rhyme.

It is quite simple for us to pick up the chant as well. Try it for yourself.

'and the evening passed and the morning came'.

It is as if Moses is teaching a song to the Israelites in order to assist in their remembering of the process of creation.

We used to sing a song that went something like, 'there was an old lady who swallowed a fly, I don't know why she swallowed a fly, perhaps she'll die'.

This same refrain came at the end of each verse as the song progressed and I wonder if we too are discovering here a marching song as the Israelites walked across the desert sand.

'and the evening passed and the morning came'.

I am hypothesizing of course. We don't know.

The Hebrew word that we have here for a day is 'yom'. The same word has also been used elsewhere in scripture to indicate a longer period of time such as an eon or an era: an unspecified period.

I find it interesting that we are given here, within the first act of creation, the advice that this was the first 'day' even before the sun and moon were created, which are two timepieces by which time has historically been measured.

The question has to be asked, how long was this day that existed before the sun rose or dropped below the horizon?

Are we hearing about a sequence of actions that needed to be remembered by rhyme and Moses used the days of the week as a simple way of learning?

It is clear that Moses wanted to bring attention to the fact that there were six periods of time, after which God rested.

God had only recently given instructions to the Israelites that they too were to rest on the sabbath day.

It is difficult to come to a firm conclusion as to whether this day - 'yom' is a precise twenty four hour day, a simple to remember rhyme or a description of longer periods of time.

We could stand our ground and argue either of the possibilities or raise another hypothesis of our own.

To do so would be foolish and destructive. At this time we can not be sure. We can only have an opinion which may or may not be correct.

Our aim is to live in unity. To argue about things that have relatively no importance would be to fall into the hands of the enemy.

In many ways it doesn't matter. What does matter is that God is telling us something through the narrative if we choose to hear Him.

We have arrived at verse four.
A foundation has been laid.

We will begin to move forward with more haste.

Chapter 2.

The days of creation.

Genesis 1:6-13 NLT
Then God said, "Let there be a space between the waters, to separate the waters of the heavens from the waters of the earth."

And that is what happened.

God made this space to separate the waters of the earth from the waters of the heavens.
God called the space "sky."

And evening passed and morning came, marking the second day.

Then God said, "Let the waters beneath the sky flow together into one place, so dry ground may appear."

And that is what happened.

God called the dry ground "land" and the waters "seas." And God saw that it was good.

Then God said, "Let the land sprout with vegetation—every sort of seed-bearing plant, and trees that grow seed-bearing fruit. These seeds will then produce the kinds of plants and trees from which they came."

And that is what happened.

The land produced vegetation - all sorts of seed-bearing plants, and trees with seed-bearing fruit. Their seeds produced plants and trees of the same kind. And God saw that it was good.

And evening passed and morning came, marking the third day.

We have begun a journey through the book of Genesis.

We have seen that there can be many ways that we might interpret the information that we have been given.

What we know is that God has something that He wants us to be a part of.

It is for us to get involved in His story.

I won't do this for each section of scripture we come across, but in these initial verses I have laid out the text in the form of a song or a poem.

We have looked at the repetitive phrase, '*And evening passed and morning came*' and wondered if this might be the chorus of a marching song.

After the first day is described we can discover two other repetitive phrases.

After each new description of the creative process we read the phrase. '*And that is what happened*'.

Then we read,
'And God saw that it was good'.

I may well be completely wrong but I can't help but recall the chants on the football terraces of similar short phrases.

If this is a marching song then it might well have spurred the tired feet of some lagging Israelite or struck fear and terror into the heart of an opposing army.

We do not know and so I will leave you to come to your own prayerful conclusion.

We read that the first act of creation after the introduction of light is the separation of the waters.

We have discovered earlier that God's Spirit hovered over the waters and now God separated them. There is a separation of the waters of heaven and the waters on earth.

Incidentally the heaven here isn't the heaven where God lives but a description of the higher regions above the earth.

God called this separation between the waters, sky.

When we read later about the flood that came upon the earth in Noah's time, we find that it is these waters of heaven that come down to assist in drowning the land.

The second day is complete.

It is on the third day that God caused the waters below the sky to come together in one place.

Before this the waters were not in one place but there was no land either. So where was the water before they came together?

Possibly it was in the form of a mist or steam that was over the earth. Scientists suggest that the earth was warm and took some time to cool.

The waters came together and land appeared.

This is the only time in the creation process that we read about the introduction of water and so now might be a good time to talk about rain.

We don't read about it raining on earth until the time of the flood that Noah and his contemporaries experienced much later.

It is only then that the waters that are stored above the sky are let loose on the earth.

We will find out in chapter two of Genesis that before man was created there was no rain but the earth was watered by springs that came up from the ground.

Once land has been established God created vegetation, plants and trees. Each plant and tree produced seed and fruit of its own in order to reproduce itself.

The self reproduction process is something that God organised very early on.

We too are created in order to reproduce fruit of our own kind.

That is the case in our natural reproduction and spiritual reproduction - both.

Our fruit is within us. Whether that be good fruit or bad fruit is dependent upon our willingness to be pruned by the gardener.

After the refrain *'and that is what happened'*
Moses again repeated the process of what had happened.

The end of the third day.

When we read scripture it is very easy to have a fixed opinion upon what we're reading that is perhaps related to something that we have been taught as a child or by a teacher or having read a commentary we have previously enjoyed.

I fall into this trap, as we all do. It is difficult for us to read without putting aside previous ideas and also having an ear to hear what Father might be wanting to teach us.

Father is wanting to speak to us through all types of mediums and experiences.

Reading the bible is only one source of understanding and often we can learn something completely new and different from the same scripture that has previously revealed something to us.

Having an open mind is crucial if we are to grow and to mature to become sons and daughters of God.

Chapter 3.

Let lights appear.

Genesis 1:14-23 NLT
Then God said, "Let lights appear in the sky to separate the day from the night. Let them be signs to mark the seasons, days, and years.
Let these lights in the sky shine down on the earth."

And that is what happened.

God made two great lights - the larger one to govern the day, and the smaller one to govern the night. He also made the stars.
God set these lights in the sky to light the earth, to govern the day and night, and to separate the light from the darkness.

And God saw that it was good.

And evening passed and morning came, marking the fourth day.

Then God said, "Let the waters swarm with fish and other life. Let the skies be filled with birds of every kind."

So God created great sea creatures and every living thing that scurries and swarms in the water, and every sort of bird—each producing offspring of the same kind.

And God saw that it was good.

Then God blessed them, saying, "Be fruitful and multiply. Let the fish fill the seas, and let the birds multiply on the earth."

And evening passed and morning came, marking the fifth day.

When we read the account of God's creation in the book of Genesis it might be easy for us to come to the conclusion that it has been written by a person with a primitive mind; by a person with little understanding of a modern understanding of how the world works.

This is not necessarily the case.

If the author of Genesis is Moses, and there is no reason to suppose otherwise, we must rethink that conclusion.

Moses was a man who was educated within Pharaoh's courts of Egypt.

The Egyptians may not have been in control of a full understanding of the universe, any more than we are today, but they had a better understanding of the skies than Moses has given us in saying that the sun and the moon and the stars are simply lights that God has placed in the sky.

Moses would have had a lot of Egyptian knowledge with regards to the manner that the sun moves around in relation to the moon and how the stars in their constellations relate to each other.

Each notable star and constellation in the sky would have had a name and purpose according to Egyptian scientific teaching in addition to the religious teaching that was associated with the skies.

And yet in his description of the forming of the skies Moses simply lets us know that God placed lights in the sky.

God placed one large light, the sun, to govern the day and one smaller light to govern the night. He also placed many smaller lights and these are all there to be for signs to mark the seasons, days, and years.

Moses has limited his description of the skies for a purpose. This may be because he was concentrating on fitting simple ideas into the verse of an easy to remember song or poem, or perhaps because under the guidance of God's Spirit that was all God wanted him to tell us.

The point of his verse is that God has placed the constellations in the heavens purposefully for us.

They are not there to be worshipped but to give us information.

The Israelites learnt about the meanings that are held within the stars and the constellations. Astronomy was a subject that was taught at school.

When they were taken to Babylon into captivity it was the Israelites who taught the wise men of Babylon about the art and knowledge of the stars.

Consequently many years later when a particularly bright star was seen in the sky in relation to the placing of other constellations there were certain wise men who were able to decipher the meaning of those signs and travelled to bring gifts to the Saviour who was born in Bethlehem.

Being able to understand the reading of the signs in the sky however is not the same as the demonic act of astrology which leads to fortune telling.

Purporting to be able to see into the future by any means is a counterfeit teaching of the enemy, as is any form of witchcraft or magic, and is forbidden.

God has produced land and water, vegetation, trees and plants and placed the sun, moon and stars in the sky, everything is ready now for life to be introduced on earth.

Day four is complete.

Now, at the perfect time, God introduced the fish that swim in the sea and birds that fly in the sky.

Just as the plants and trees produced fruit and seed so too God has designed the fish and birds to reproduce their own kind.

At the arrival of life - fish and birds, God spoke again.

God blessed the fish and birds and told them to multiply and to fill the earth.

Although man attempts to undermine God's word, the fish and birds are still under the same instruction to multiply and to fill the earth today.

God's word cannot be put aside or overridden, it will accomplish what it has set out to achieve.

We may worry and fret about the end of the world or the decline of certain creatures and animals within it but God's word will not change.

We have a responsibility to enable God's word to produce rather than work against it.

There are many selfish actions that we individually take that undermine God's word.

There is a need for us to look again at some of the things that we do that undermine God's blessing in this respect.

The end of the fifth day.

Chapter 4.

The sixth day.

Genesis 1:24-31 NLT
Then God said, "Let the earth produce every sort of animal, each producing offspring of the same kind—livestock, small animals that scurry along the ground, and wild animals."

And that is what happened.

God made all sorts of wild animals, livestock, and small animals, each able to produce offspring of the same kind.

And God saw that it was good.

God's creation is gathering pace now. We are on God's sixth day.

Again God spoke.

The fish and birds are doing well. God is pleased with them and now He introduced wild animals, livestock and small animals.

I love the way that Moses has described the small animals as *'the ones that scurry along the ground'*.

I can imagine that the Israelites, in their tents, had some experience of *'small animals that scurry along the ground'*.

It is important when we read and discuss the word of God that we bear in mind that it is written under the guidance of God's Spirit.

It might be easy for us to take a particular scripture and, in our lack of understanding, criticise or dispute or even doubt its authenticity.

It is true that there may be some flaws in the way that scripture has been interpreted for us.

It is also true that there is much that is yet to be revealed to us within its pages.

What we can't do, in our study of scripture, is to deny God's hand and purposes for us within what we read.

The author has described the introduction of different kinds of animals.

The crescendo of creation is becoming louder and larger.

We are not invited to analyse these introductions or we might stop to enquire as to the nature of the livestock that is introduced in Moses verses.

Moses might have taken some time to teach us that the tame or domesticated animals - livestock, were once wild.

He may also have taken time to explain that it is man, who has not yet been introduced into the creation, that managed the tame animals.

If man had not already been on the scene, to what purpose were there livestock and why and how were they tame?

If man had no need of clothing or meat to what purpose were the livestock, tame animals, put to?

Or did Moses use the term 'livestock' to fit in with the rhythm of a poem?

All of these questions arise and others also.

It is possible and perhaps even likely that God prepared domesticated animals for the arrival of man on the scene.

We have a choice to make. Do we take the scriptures as they are laid out; take them at face value and realise that God can and does order as He pleases?

Do we assess as to whether God, through Moses, is giving us an overall picture of the process of creation in order to teach us something of His guidance through the process of and many other things besides?

Or do we throw the whole book out of the window as so much made up nonsense as many do?

Or do we come to another conclusion altogether?

What we can't do is to simply bury our head in the sand and ignore the apparent anomalies that occur within the dialogue.

We have a responsibility to give an explanation to others who might inquire about these things and how we approach that might be crucial in how they spend eternity.

It is our own responsibility to prayerfully receive answers on these matters in order for us to give an account.

It is true that there are occasional difficulties with the translation of scripture, - translators are human and make mistakes as we all do.

Under the guidance of God's Spirit we can discover these and realise the truth.

God's Spirit has given us scripture to reveal Himself to us. We need to hear what God is saying to us within the pages for ourselves.

With regards to the book of Genesis I believe that we have the choice of taking it as we read it; to realise that God is God and can bring anything into being as He pleases at a whim.

Or we might come to the conclusion that there is a different type of teaching within its pages.

God is from the beginning. He existed before time. He is behind every creative act and will be for all eternity.

Our understanding of Him and His actions are limited to say the very least. We can never comprehend even a small fragment of God.

Perhaps this fact is behind the writings of Moses. No matter how much explanation and detail, we could never fully enter into the magnitude of God, His purposes or His character.

Moses, in awe, is saying, "I can't describe what or how God created the universes". He simply writes, 'this is what happened, isn't God amazing!'.

What we can't do is use scripture to suit our own mind set or allow apparent and insignificant anomalies to cause division among us. To do so would be playing into the hands of the enemy who loves to create division.

God has made animals and He must have been really pleased with how things were coming along, I would have been!

In a final flourish and touch of genius, as if to place the cherry on the top of the most amazing cake ever produced, God made man and woman.

We will look at these final introductions to creation next but it is worth noting here that God has not yet given the creatures or man the authority to eat meat within His creation.

The plants, nuts, seeds and fruit are all made freely available to them but no meat is to be eaten.

We are at the end of the sixth day and at the introduction of man God said, "It is very good".

Chapter 5.

The Arrival of man and woman.

Genesis 1: 27-31
Then God said, "Let us make human beings in our image, to be like us. They will reign over the fish in the sea, the birds in the sky, the livestock, all the wild animals on the earth, and the small animals that scurry along the ground."

So God created human beings in his own image. In the image of God he created them; male and female he created them.

Then God blessed them and said, "Be fruitful and multiply. Fill the earth and govern it. Reign over the fish in the sea, the birds in the sky, and all the animals that scurry along the ground."
Then God said, "Look! I have given you every seed-bearing plant throughout the earth and all the fruit trees for your food.

And I have given every green plant as food for all the wild animals, the birds in the sky, and the small animals that scurry along the ground - everything that has life."

And that is what happened.

Then God looked over all he had made, and he saw that it was very good!

And evening passed and morning came, marking the sixth day.

At the end of the last creative act we see that God's creation is crowned with the entry of man onto the scene.

At which point God said, *"It is very good"*.

Previously God had declared at each act of creation that *'it was good'*. Now man and woman are on the scene and God declared, *'it is very good'*.

I expect to hear a drum roll at this point.

Creation is completed.

There is an inclination in the world today for us to believe that we are on the earth as a secondary issue; a perhaps unnecessary and even unwanted addition to nature and the animals.

God wants us to know that this is very much not the case. We are God's primary concern; we are the icing on the cake and it is because of, and for the sake of us that God created the universe and not vice versa.

God enforced this understanding by giving the first man and woman the authority to govern His creation.

God has built a beautiful universe. It is now up and running and working perfectly and God has chosen to hand the whole array of perfection that He has tirelessly and patiently brought into existence over to mankind to manage.

Can we even begin to imagine the trust, faith, expectancy, confidence and capability that God has in us?

He gave the first man and woman authority to rule over the fish in the sea, the birds, the wild animals, the livestock and the small animals *'that scurry along on the ground'*.

God sees each one of us in the same way as He viewed the first. We are each one of us, unique and perfect and cherished by God who has made us because He purposed us to be born and for us to be one with Him.

God was conversing with Himself as He created. We read that, *God said, "Let us make human beings in our image, to be like us.*

This must have been quite a conversation to have. We take such little notice of those few words.

God has options.

We could have been created as the animals and other creatures, to be managed for reproductive purposes or to be servants, at God's beck and call.

God said, *"Let us make human beings in our image, to be like us"*.

God designed us differently and also gave us free will because He wanted us to be a part of Him.

We are not designed to be held at arm's length or at some place apart from God but to be like Him in our ways, thoughts, understanding, management and creative abilities and so much more.

God has made us in His image.

There is something about us that has the nature of God.

God has not said this about any other aspect of His creation. We are different.

Being made in 'the image of God' is a huge subject and we will perhaps discuss this another time.

We do not all look alike and so we are not discussing purely external features but aspects of intellect, morality, compassion, the sanctity of life, the ability to love, grieve etc.

Since our creation we have become marred by sin. The pure image of God in us needs to be redeemed.

Our thoughts, motivations and concepts are flawed and fall far short of God's creation, but the image, although flawed and in need of redemption, is still there.

Jesus came into the world, suffered and died in order for that redemption to become possible for us. Such is God's amazing and everlasting love for each one of us.

Those who believe that God is not a triune God may want to take note of these verses as God discusses the creation.

God established many things at the beginning of His creation.

Genesis is a book that lays down foundations for us.

One of those foundations is found in the very first verses as we read about Father, Son and Spirit and also confirmed here as God discussed His plans.

He very purposefully used the word *'us'* twice in His conversation He refers to 'us' and 'our' - *"Let us make human beings in our image, to be like us".*

God made Adam and Eve on the sixth day.

Are we looking at six twenty four hour periods, six specific periods of time, six ages, a sixth verse in Moses song or poem or the fact that Moses was teaching the

Israelites about the next day which is the seventh and sabbath day?

We don't know for sure.

But it is appropriate that God made man on the sixth day.

We find in scripture that numbers have specific meanings. It is good to look out for them because, more often than not, God is wanting us to understand something through the number that has been used.

The number six is the number of man.

Number seven is the number of God's perfection. The number six is one short of seven and indicates man's attempts at reaching God and inevitably falling short of that target.

If you are reading these pages on a chapter per day basis, tomorrow we begin looking at the summing up of creation and the beginnings of the life of man and woman.

Chapter 6.

The seventh day

Gen 2:1-7
So the creation of the heavens and the earth and everything in them was completed. On the seventh day God had finished his work of creation, so he rested from all his work. And God blessed the seventh day and declared it holy, because it was the day when he rested from all his work of creation.

This is the account of the creation of the heavens and the earth.

When the Lord God made the earth and the heavens, neither wild plants nor grains were growing on the earth. For the Lord God had not yet sent rain to water the earth, and there were no people to cultivate the soil. Instead, springs came up from the ground and watered all the land.

Then the Lord God formed the man from the dust of the ground. He breathed the breath of life into the man's nostrils, and the man became a living person.

With verse four of Genesis in chapter two the style of writing changes.

The rhythmic, repetitive, poetic form that we experienced in chapter one has moved into being a more straightforward teaching style.

Verses one, two and three of Genesis chapter two finish off the seven day sequence of creation that is laid out for us in chapter one.

It is worth noting here at the beginning of Genesis, where we can read for ourselves that the thread at the end of one chapter has spilt into the next, that the chapters, verses and subheadings that we read in our Bibles are not given in the original text.

They have been added into the Bible by the translators in order to assist our understanding of what we read.

The translators have also added punctuation into the text where they believe it is required - fullstops, comma's, colons, semi-colons, question marks, speech marks etc.

None of these are in the original text.

Some of which are helpful, others are not as helpful.

There is one particular comma that the translators have placed in scripture that I find extremely annoying that has caused much misunderstanding of scripture for centuries.

This is not the place to discuss that one but there will be an opportunity to find out about it when we move on to the life of Enoch who was the father of Methuselah.

The animals and man are created on day six, and on day seven God rested.

Creation is complete.

This series of events completes a seven day cycle. God called the seventh day the Sabbath - a day of rest.

We don't read that God has ever begun a new day after the seventh day of creation and so we can assume that God is still resting: we too are still living in God's Sabbath day.

The Sabbath day means many things to different people.

To the devout religious leaders in the time of Jesus it meant that nothing that could be classified as work was allowed to be carried out.

This included healing on the Sabbath, walking too far a distance, preparing food and many other nonsensical things.

Jesus mocked their understanding of what they thought the Sabbath meant.

Although the Sabbath was a Saturday, there are religious types today who have a similar view to those religious leaders in Jesus' time as to what is allowed to be done on a Sunday.

The truth is that the Mosaic laws that governed the Sabbath day that God gave to Moses were only a shadow; a picture or foretelling of the eternal Sabbath that was brought about by the sacrifice of Jesus who died to redeem us from the law of sin and death.

We who have come into God's Kingdom live in God's eternal Sabbath: His day of rest is always with us.

We begin verse four of chapter two with the words, *'this is the account of the creation of the heaven's and the earth'.*

The verse gives the impression that what is coming next will be the account of the creation.

The verse leads me to ask why there was a previous account of creation and why are we given two accounts?

We will look at this question shortly.

We are told here that before plants and animals and people were on the earth, before rain had fallen, the earth was watered by springs that came up from under the earth.

Indeed we don't read about rain until much later, when God decided to bring a flood upon the earth in Noah's time.

Then the heavens were opened and the springs that were under the earth were let loose.

Then God made man from the dust of the earth, breathed 'life' into him and he became a living being.

There can be no denying that there is some considerable disagreement with regards to this verse.

Are we being given the picture of a one off miraculous event in which God made a man or is Moses giving us a final picture of what has been a long process of evolution?

Either answer might be the correct one.

My own conclusion arises from the events that occurred after the resurrection of Jesus.

Jesus was in an upper room with His disciples when He 'breathed upon them'.

Then he breathed on them and said, "Receive the Holy Spirit.
John 20:22 NLT

Paul explained further when he tells us that those who have received the Holy Spirit are a 'new creation'.

This means that anyone who belongs to Christ has become a new person. The old life is gone; a new life has begun!
2 Corinthians 5:17 NLT

The wording within these two verses is very similar to the wording we have in Genesis where God breathed life into the man and *'he became a living being'.*

We can conclude from the account of the creation in Genesis that God oversaw the development of all of His creation.

God spoke it into existence, watched over its progression, perhaps nudging it along when needed, sowed seed, patiently awaited the arrival of some event before initiating another burst of life.

It is true to say, in either scenario, that man was born from the *'dust of the ground'.*

It is possible that there was a time when man reached a point of comprehension; an understanding or awareness of a creator and then God stepped in and 'breathed' supernatural life into Him; man became a new creation.

The fact that we, who are now one with Christ, are also a 'new creation' doesn't mean that we didn't exist before that transformation. Of course we did.

But we are now a new creation.

We don't celebrate the old however, because the new has come.

We can apply the same principle to the 'new man' in Moses' account of the creation.

My views are not necessarily correct of course. God may have taken the dust of the earth, created the animals, built a man and then breathed life into Him, exactly as we have read, within a twenty four hour day.

God is God and is able to do as He pleases.

I am well aware of all of the miraculous, spontaneous and immediate acts that God carries out.

My understanding of God though is not one of immediacy or speed.

I see a greater act of love and care and the immensity of God in a patient laying down of minerals over the years and a gradual development of life.

When we come into God's kingdom we are not immediately transformed into a perfect being: one who is perfectly upright and righteous, never making mistakes and being full of wisdom.

God could wave a magic wand and we become perfection in seconds but He doesn't encourage our new life in that way.

Our growth to become fully mature sons and daughters of God is achieved over a period of time by learning and development.

Those are my prayerful thoughts on the process of creation. You must hear what God's Spirit is saying to you for yourself.

I had intended to get to verse twenty today!

We must hurry along now but I think there is so much disagreement with regards to these verses that whilst we need to learn to be tolerant towards those who have a different understanding and to put aside our preconceived ideas, we also need to gather as much information about what is written that we are able to in order to prayerfully come to our own understanding.

Chapter 7.

Eden

Genesis 2:7-20
Then the Lord God planted a garden in Eden in the east,
and there he placed the man he had made. The Lord
God made all sorts of trees grow up from the ground -
trees that were beautiful and that produced delicious
fruit. In the middle of the garden he placed the tree of
life and the tree of the knowledge of good and evil.

A river flowed from the land of Eden, watering the
garden and then dividing into four branches.
The first branch, called the Pishon, flowed around the
entire land of Havilah, where gold is found. The gold of
that land is exceptionally pure; aromatic resin and onyx
stone are also found there.
The second branch, called the Gihon, flowed around the
entire land of Cush.
The third branch, called the Tigris, flowed east of the
land of Asshur.
The fourth branch is called the Euphrates.

The Lord God placed the man in the Garden of Eden to
tend and watch over it. But the Lord God warned him,
"You may freely eat the fruit of every tree in the garden -
except the tree of the knowledge of good and evil. If you
eat its fruit, you are sure to die."

Then the Lord God said, "It is not good for the man to be alone. I will make a helper who is just right for him."

Verse 19 So the Lord God formed from the ground all the wild animals and all the birds of the sky. He brought them to the man to see what he would call them, and the man chose a name for each one.
He gave names to all the livestock, all the birds of the sky, and all the wild animals.

But still there was no helper just right for him.

God planted a garden in the east and placed the man in it.

There were all sorts of trees there that produced delicious fruit.

In the middle of the garden He placed the tree of life and the tree of the knowledge of good and evil.

Unlike the previous plants and trees that God has produced these two trees are not trees that reproduce themselves.

Whether these were physical trees or whether they symbolise something else that was in existence at that time we are not told.

We know that Adam is specifically told not to eat of the fruit of the tree of good and evil.

God further advises Adam that if he did eat the fruit of that tree he would die.

The garden was a good place to be. Within it there was everything that man could need.

There was a river that flowed through the garden that had four branches. This is not the normal idea that we have when we think of a garden.

We are describing an enormous area of land. The great Euphrates is just one of the four branches of the river that flowed through it.

Then God said, *"it is not good for man to be alone, I will make a helper who is just right for him"*.

God had declared over everything that He had made previously that *"it was good"*. Now God has seen that man is alone and He declared *"it is not good"*.

So God brought all of the animals in front of the man for him to name.

We can be pretty sure that God realised that Adam wasn't going to find a suitable helper for him amongst the animals, so what is happening here?

When we place a name upon someone or something we are announcing our responsibility for that thing.

Here God is giving Adam the responsibility for all the life that He has created.

God also needed Adam to appreciate that there is no compatibility between man and the animals.

Here in verse nineteen and twenty we have, what appears to be, another of those small discrepancies in either the scripture or the translation of the scripture.

The word 'so' means 'as a consequence of'.

The word 'then' means 'afterwards'.

I have studied several different translations of these verses and the majority of them give the reading that the animals and birds and livestock are made from the dust of the ground *'as a consequence of'* the need for Adam to have a companion.

But in chapter one we have read that the man was created after the animals and birds.

In chapter one we have man and woman created together, in chapter two we have man created first.

In many ways it doesn't matter which came first but I like to have these things explained. I don't like loose ends.

Someone might come along one day and ask me why there are apparent discrepancies in scripture and I would like to have an answer for them.

If chapter one is simply a marching song or a way of teaching the Israelites about the construction of the universe that Moses chose to write down for us we can understand the manner in which it has been written - Moses needed to fit words into verses and hopefully get them to rhyme.

But is the answer that simple?

I have read papers that explicitly state that the new international version and other versions of the Bible, that suggest that the animals and birds had already been created by God, and were then brought before the man, as we read in the script in chapter two, cannot be correct as the original text doesn't allow for it to be translated in that way.

So that would have been an easy explanation, but that has been squashed.

There has been the explanation that God saw that the man was lonely and so created a further and different group of animals for him to name, other than those He had previously created.

This idea too has no real foundation and seems an unnecessary and unwarranted addition to the story.

The answer seems to be that there is no answer.

The translators, and wiser men than I am, have struggled with the text for many years without coming to a satisfactory conclusion.

But now I have raised it, we must come to a conclusion of some sort.

I personally believe that chapter one is laid out as it is because God and Moses wanted to teach the Isaelites and us about God's hand in creation. There is order and a master plan involved from the very beginning.

Chapter two is laid out differently because God wants us to learn something else from the events and the order that they were introduced in the creation is not relevant for us.

I have another additional explanation in that the bible is God's word.

Here in chapters one and two we have two different versions of creation.

I would be surprised if we could ever in a million trillion years ever really understand even one version of all that was involved in the creation of the universe.

It is more than likely that both versions are correct and we have simply misunderstood what God is saying about it.

There is also the possibility that these two versions were written by two individuals who had a different revelation from God.

This is something that frequently happens today. Do we need to accept that God speaks to one person in one way and another person in a different way?

I also wonder if God is suggesting that our lives need to be built upon faith rather than our own understanding?

Faith in God's word, whether that is the written word of the Bible or His word in our ear today, is the foundation for living in God's kingdom.

Is the apparent confusion in the text a first lesson in faith that has been placed in front of us?

The easiest way out of the difficulty is to assume that God brought all of the animals and birds that He had previously created before the man but apparently the original text doesn't allow for this reading.

Perhaps the true answer is that the evolutionists are correct - that man and animals developed in conjunction with each other under God's guiding hand.

I suspect that if it were an important issue we would have a definitive explanation.

We will look at the birth of Eve next.

Chapter 8.

Eve.

Genesis 2:9-25.
The Lord God made all sorts of trees grow up from the ground trees that were beautiful and that produced delicious fruit. In the middle of the garden he placed the tree of life and the tree of the knowledge of good and evil.

The Lord God placed the man in the Garden of Eden to tend and watch over it. But the Lord God warned him, "You may freely eat the fruit of every tree in the garden - except the tree of the knowledge of good and evil. If you eat its fruit, you are sure to die."

Then the Lord God said, "It is not good for the man to be alone. I will make a helper who is just right for him."

So the Lord God formed from the ground all the wild animals and all the birds of the sky. He brought them to the man to see what he would call them, and the man chose a name for each one. He gave names to all the livestock, all the birds of the sky, and all the wild animals. But still there was no helper just right for him.

So the Lord God caused the man to fall into a deep sleep. While the man slept, the Lord God took out one of the man's ribs and closed up the opening. Then the Lord

God made a woman from the rib, and he brought her to the man.

"At last!" the man exclaimed. "This one is bone from my bone, and flesh from my flesh! She will be called 'woman,' because she was taken from 'man.

'" This explains why a man leaves his father and mother and is joined to his wife, and the two are united into one.

Now the man and his wife were both naked, but they felt no shame.

We have discovered, as Adam has, that there is no compatibility to be had between man and the other creatures that God has made.

God saw that this was not a good situation for Adam to be in. Adam needed a helper - a companion.

It is significant that God said, *"it is not good for man to be alone"*.

It seems to me that we have two options when reading about the creation of Eve.

We can read it as the description of a single event that occurred after Adam was walking with God - God put Adam into a deep sleep, took one of his ribs or a part of his side, modelled a woman from it and breathed life into her.

Or we can read it as a teaching aid to assist us in understanding the relationship between God, man and woman.

Biologists can teach us that two different sexual species occurred some 2.5 billion years ago.

These species are called *eukaryotic* and were the first creatures that required two opposite sexes in order to mate and reproduce.

I can't give a definitive answer as to which view to take and my opinion will not help you if I am mistaken.

If, or when, the Lord chooses to give us an insight into these things we will know more.

What we do know for sure is that God saw that it was not good for man to be alone. It is necessary that there are two seperate sexes - male and female.

The enemy, who is satan, would attempt to undermine and confuse the plans of God but he is destined to fail.

It must have been some time before God introduced the woman to Adam.

I like Adam's exclamation - *"at last!"*.

This small comment tells us a lot.

1. Adam had been on his own and was looking for a companion.
2. The introduction of Eve was a new thing for him.
3. It was a long awaited event.

We can ask some questions:

Was Adam alone because he was the only man on earth or because He had been taken away from others to be a new creation and then placed 'in the garden', or was 'Adam' a group of people?

The latter doesn't seem likely if there were no women to assist in creating other people.

Was Eve created from Adam's side or is she another female that had come to a realisation of God as Adam may have?

Some of us are joined with a partner who perhaps doesn't know God and we can share Adam's "at last" when our partners come into the same relationship, or indeed when anyone comes into a relationship with God.

We might consider that Adam may have been alone for hundreds of years before the woman was introduced, but we are not told this.

Adam prophesied over the woman.

"This one is bone from my bone, and flesh from my flesh! She will be called 'woman', because she was taken from 'man'.

'"This explains why a man leaves his father and mother and is joined to his wife, and the two are united into one".

Adam described her as 'this one', meaning this new creation of God (that isn't one of the animals).

God wants us to understand that the woman was taken from man.

This isn't to do with a hierarchy. Man is not in any way superior to the female. Both are created to have the same relationship with God and to be on an equal footing.

We are joined together to be submitted to each other and not for one to be inferior or of lesser concern.

We are placed together to serve each other's best interests in love, whatever that might mean in our own individual situations.

Eve was taken from man to provide us with an understanding that man is not complete alone. There is something in a woman that will complete him. And indeed, there is something in man that will complete the woman.

It is presumably Moses or some other person who has added the last sentence attributed to Adam, because if Adam and Eve are the first and only people on earth they would not have known of fathers and mothers.

It is another difficult text to explain.

If they are the first humans perhaps God gave them an understanding of parents.

They may not be the first people on earth but the first humans who were given 'new life'.

The text may have been added later.

But God wants us to know that when we become one with another we need to leave our past behind us.

This is because we are becoming a new person in unity with another. There is no room within that relationship for in-laws, fathers, mothers, brothers, sisters, uncles and aunts.

When we become joined to another the old person has gone and we have become one new person together, walking into a new future.

God introduced to Adam a woman who was 'just right for him'.

If we listen to God's Spirit we will also be introduced to a partner who is 'just right for us'.

There are occasions when we might need to change in order to become useful in a new relationship.

Our patience in allowing the Lord to prepare us towards this union will pay dividends in terms of our ability to produce good fruit from it.

There are also occasions when the union that we are in does not appear to be one that is 'just right for us'.

This is often because the Lord is requiring a change in us in order for the relationship to fit properly - we need to learn how to love unconditionally possibly.

We can be sure that the Lord does not make mistakes when He chooses the right partner for us.

We will look at the trees planted in the garden next.

Chapter 9.

Two trees.

Genesis 2:9, 15-17.
The Lord God made all sorts of trees grow up from the ground - trees that were beautiful and that produced delicious fruit.

In the middle of the garden he placed the tree of life and the tree of the knowledge of good and evil.

The Lord God placed the man in the Garden of Eden to tend and watch over it. But the Lord God warned him, "You may freely eat the fruit of every tree in the garden - except the tree of the knowledge of good and evil.

If you eat its fruit, you are sure to die."

We have all seen cartoons and read various humorous comments surrounding the story of Adam and Eve taking a bite of an apple.

These misleading stories and jokes have perhaps seriously undermined the truth behind the facts that we need to know about.

It is in the nature of the enemy to plant seeds of disbelief in an attempt to deceive us.

We need to remove these foolish ideas from our thoughts so that we can begin to establish a foundation of truth by listening to what Father is telling us.

The enemy - satan, would rather we didn't ask questions about sin and the consequences of sin.

If he can focus our minds on shallow jokes instead he has won us over.

We need to hear what Father said to Adam when He placed him in the garden.

God said, " if you eat of the fruit of the tree of knowledge of good and evil you will die".

Remember those words.

Among other various fruit bearing trees there were two trees placed in the garden.

One was the tree of life. The other was the tree of the knowledge of good and evil.

These two trees stand apart from the other trees.

God gave Adam permission to eat from any tree apart from the tree of the knowledge of good and evil.

If God didn't want Adam to eat its fruit, why was it there?

Let's look at what the tree of the knowledge of good and evil represents.

The knowledge of good and evil is something that Solomon asked God for when he became king over Israel.

So give Your servant an understanding mind and a hearing heart [with which] to judge Your people, so that I may discern between good and evil. For who is able to judge and rule this great people of Yours?"
1 Kings 3:9 AMP

The writer to the Hebrews rebuked his readers because they behaved like children, needing milk rather than eating solid food.

They were not mature and were unable to discern between good and evil.

But solid food is for the [spiritually] mature, whose senses are trained by practice to distinguish between what is morally good and what is evil.
Hebrews 5:14 AMP

The knowledge of good and evil isn't like a download of all that is bad and good. It is the ability to make mature judgments.

God placed the man and the woman in the garden as immature children that needed to learn how to manage the place that they had been given.

In the tree of the knowledge of good and evil there was a choice for them to make.

They could learn to become mature by submitting to God in His teaching which would lead them into maturity and the ability to make right judgments, or they could become autonomous, making immature decisions based upon their own, flawed knowledge.

We will discover which decision they made and how it affected the rest of mankind next but in order to understand their position we need to first understand the nature of these trees.

God realised that man without God is destined to fail.

The eating of the fruit wasn't the problem for man, it was what was behind the decision that they might make, that meant either life or death for them.

Would they submit to God's timing and training or was there a desire to bypass God - rebellion.

The tree was there for a purpose - God wanted to train them in becoming mature, making good decisions. The tree was there to aid in that aim.

God placed a temporary 'hold off' sign on the tree in order to test them. They were destined to 'become like Gods', able to judge between good and evil under God's teaching.

Would they be able to pass the test?

Or will they be tempted into bypassing God's teaching - into rebellion?

The nature of sin is rebellion towards God - trying to achieve in our own strength or limited knowledge: excluding God.

God often places tests in our own life in order to see how mature we are in making good decisions.

How do we fare in the tests that we are given?

If we make good decisions then we will move on towards maturity and perhaps win a crown and a "well done".

If we make bad decisions we are not condemned for those decisions but we will find that the same tests will come around at some time in our future until we learn to make good decisions.

Do we make our decisions based upon what we know of God and what He is telling us or are our thoughts still in tune with the world around us?

How mature or 'Christlike', are we becoming?

The second tree is the tree of life and was a tree that the man and woman were already eating from.

Notice that the tree of life has been placed at the centre of the garden.

Our tree of life is Jesus and He too must be placed in the centre of our own garden.

Whilst they lived in submission to God the tree of life was there for them in abundance for eternity.

This is also the case for us if we live in submission to God's training in our lives.

Abundant and eternal life is available for us, from the tree of life, whilst we live in submission to God's training.

We will discover next how Adam and Eve coped with their own tests.

Chapter 10.

Sin

Genesis 3: 1-24
The serpent was the shrewdest of all the wild animals the Lord God had made.

One day he asked the woman, "Did God really say you must not eat the fruit from any of the trees in the garden?" "Of course we may eat fruit from the trees in the garden," the woman replied. "It's only the fruit from the tree in the middle of the garden that we are not allowed to eat.
God said, 'You must not eat it or even touch it; if you do, you will die.'" "You won't die!" the serpent replied to the woman. "God knows that your eyes will be opened as soon as you eat it, and you will be like God, knowing both good and evil." The woman was convinced.

She saw that the tree was beautiful and its fruit looked delicious, and she wanted the wisdom it would give her. So she took some of the fruit and ate it. Then she gave some to her husband, who was with her, and he ate it, too.

At that moment their eyes were opened, and they suddenly felt shame at their nakedness. So they sewed fig leaves together to cover themselves.

When the cool evening breezes were blowing, the man and his wife heard the Lord God walking about in the garden. So they hid from the Lord God among the trees.

We have seen that God had set Adam and Eve in a garden full of good things - all that they could possibly need.

Their purpose in life is to reproduce and fill the earth with the fruit of themselves as they grow into maturity under the Lordship of God's training.

They were to become, 'like God', judging between good and evil',' as they grew up - everything that God had created had been placed under their care.

As God trained them, in time He would also test them on their decision making abilities.

Although scripture often depicts satan as a serpent, we are not told in these verses that it was satan who spoke to Eve.

We are informed that the serpent was the shrewdest of the animals and apparently he could speak, or at least, he could make himself understood by Eve.

His first words are in the form of a question designed to undermine God's words.
Was this a thought process as we sometimes experience when the enemy attempts to deceive us?

"Did God really say"?.......

It was God's prerogative to test His children in His own time but, in rebellion, the serpent preempted God's plan and attacked whilst they were still very weak, as he still does today, preying on the weak and vulnerable.

Eve should have told him to clear off and to stop undermining God's word but instead she decided to reply.

Eve started out well with her reply, supporting what God had said, but the enemy was not to be put off so easily and came back with a direct contradiction.

"You will not die" he said, "what God has told you is not true, you have misunderstood, God is stopping you from having something good".

Eve was convinced. She could see that the fruit was good and so her reasoning was, "why would God not want me to have it"?

She was on the slippery slope of questioning God's decisions.

On the face of it Eve's thinking was reasonable, she wanted the wisdom that the fruit would give her and, after all, God was training her to become wise.

But she is conveniently forgetting the overriding words of God, which were, "not to eat it".

Eve took the fruit and gave some to Adam who was there, and 'immediately their eyes were opened'.

They felt shame at their nakedness and made leaves to cover themselves.

Adam and Eve were able to judge between good and evil but their judgement was now flawed and it proved fatal for them.

In having their eyes opened they realised how utterly lost they were, outside and apart from God.

What a dreadful feeling that must have been. How full of remorse, sorrow and grief they must have felt.

I don't think we can ever really appreciate the sense of loss they must have experienced, having lived perpetually in the presence of God and for that life to vanish in an instant.

Their nakedness wasn't to do with their lack of clothes, although that is what is illustrated, but their very existence. They now have nothing and realise how lost they are without God.

They attempt, unsuccessfully, to patch themselves up with leaves that will very soon wilt and die.

Their knowledge of judging between good and evil has placed them in a very difficult position.

They are lost and a righteous, holy God is calling to them in the evening breeze. How will they respond?

Previously they had met with God, chatted and enjoyed each other's company without a thought, but now rebellion or sin has got in the way of that union.

They were afraid and hid. Already their flawed judgement is deceiving them.

It is a good job that God knows what is going on and never stops loving them, and us.

Adam was given authority over all of the animals and yet he chose to submit to the advice of a serpent.

This decision has left us in a world where we hide from God.

There is an unbridgeable gulf between God, who lives in holy righteousness, and man who lives increasingly in a fallen state of sin.

The two can never be joined as one again. Sin will now eternally reign in the life of man - such is the loss for creation that occurred here in the garden.

These are the horrendous facts that the enemy attempts to conceal from us with humorous jokes and cartoons.

I do hope that God has a plan.

Let us find out next.

Chapter 11.

Judgement

Genesis 3:9-16
Then the Lord God called to the man, "Where are you?"
He replied, "I heard you walking in the garden, so I hid. I
was afraid because I was naked." "Who told you that
you were naked?" the Lord God asked. "Have you eaten
from the tree whose fruit I commanded you not to eat?"
The man replied, "It was the woman you gave me who
gave me the fruit, and I ate it."

Then the Lord God asked the woman, "What have you
done?" "The serpent deceived me," she replied. "That's
why I ate it."
Then the Lord God said to the serpent, "Because you
have done this, you are cursed more than all animals,
domestic and wild.
You will crawl on your belly, groveling in the dust as long
as you live.

And I will cause hostility between you and the woman,
and between your offspring and her offspring.
He will strike your head, and you will strike his heel."

Then he said to the woman, "I will sharpen the pain of
your pregnancy, and in pain you will give birth.

And you will desire to control your husband, but he will
rule over you. "

The Lord asked Adam two questions:

"Who told you about your nakedness"? and, "have you done something I told you not to"?

From the beginning the Lord told Adam that the day he ate of that tree he would die. There was no confusion about what Adam had been told.

It is quite surprising how quickly the change in Adam became clear and what a difference that change was.

Adam's first response is to look for an excuse; a way out of his problem.

Who can he blame?

He began his response by blaming first the woman and then the Lord. "It was the woman you gave me, she gave it to me to eat".

The Lord doesn't take time to remind Adam that it was He who had told him not to eat it or to take Adam's accusation seriously but asked the woman a similar question to the one He asked Adam, *what have you done"?*

The woman, following Adam's lead, looked frantically for someone else to blame. *"The serpent deceived me, that's why I ate it".*

We often follow a similar line when we are in trouble, failing to accept responsibility for our own bad judgment.

The Lord didn't waste time reasoning with them, they are aware of the devastating result of their actions and will learn to accept their responsibility in that, but immediately set about putting a restoration process in place.

There is a need for both judgement and restoration.

The Lord spoke truth into the situation.

His words explained the result of the actions of the serpent, the man and the woman, for the present and into the future. He declared a good outcome and final victory for His children and eternal failure and destruction for the serpent.

It is important to notice that the Lord didn't ask the serpent what he had done or why, the Lord knew his nature and He gave him no opportunity to lie.

We don't know that prior to this incident the serpent walked upright, he may have always crawled on his belly but from now on he would always continue to do so.

This may be a reference to the fact that some animals had changed from crawling to walking on legs. The serpent can not expect to be able to do this; he would always crawl on his belly and, as we know, he still does.

The serpent is cursed more than any other animal, domestic or wild.

There will be continual hostility between the serpent and the woman, between her offspring and his offspring.

The Lord concluded His address to the serpent by declaring his final outcome.

"The offspring of the woman will strike his head, even though the serpent would strike his heel".

We can experience the continual biting at our heels of the serpent as he attempts to pull us down.

Jesus too was continually harassed by his biting but satan's head was struck a death blow when Jesus overcame him by giving His own life as a sacrifice in order to redeem us.

The serpent had no say in his judgement, there is no place of reply for him and we hear no more of him in that form again.

The Lord addressed Eve next and explained the result of what she had done.

We have been encouraged historically to read the words of the Lord to Adam and Eve in terms of a fierce anger; words spoken in wrath and punishment for the sin they have committed but I would ask you to look again at the content and take a different view.

What Adam and Eve had done will have a poisonous effect on all of creation. Sin will slowly spread and alter all of the good things that the Lord brought into being.

There is little at this time that the Lord can do to reverse that situation but will seek to bring about an eventual restoration, one that will bring glory to Jesus.

The Lord looked for a way to enable the man and woman to live in the fallen situation that they had brought upon themselves.

He offered words of hope, vision for the future and assistance in the new place they are in.

The Lord explained to the woman that childbirth, which is the hope of the future, would become more painful.

This is a difficult verse to read if we have assumed that Eve has no personal knowledge of childbirth.

Do we jump to the conclusion that Eve must have had children if her chidbearing will get more difficult?

I believe that the Lord was referring to the difficulty of childbearing becoming worse in the future of mankind.

This isn't so much a warning for Eve but for future generations.

If we wonder why childbearing is both difficult and painful, more so for some than others, we can look back at the reason this has become so.

This word from the Lord referred not only to the pain of childbearing itself but also the difficulty that many couples have in conceiving, which has become a common issue.

The answer on both levels is to look to Jesus who has redeemed us from those curses that entered the world.

We can now be set free from the difficulties surrounding childbirth, and every other curse, by working with Him to overcome the works of the enemy in our lives.

The Lord also explained the new conflicts that Eve, and us, would need to be aware of and to overcome.

"And you will desire to control your husband, but he will rule over you. "

Some versions translate this as, *"your desire and longing will be for your husband".*

The desire to *'rule over'* would replace the desire to please each other.

The desire for the Lord would be replaced by a desire for 'the man'.

Love encourages us to submit to each other

Love encourages us to seek the good of others.

The desire to *'rule over'* would replace the desire to please each other.

There is a great desire today to 'rule over' rather than to do everything in love. We enjoy being in control.

Being in control is not the place we are born to be.

This is not how we are made but is a consequence of sin.

Before sin entered the world the man and the woman each had a desire for and access to the Lord.

The woman's source of life was God, as was the man's.

Sin has twisted this natural relationship so that now, often, the woman looks to the man as her life source.

This in turn creates pressure on the man to carry a responsibility that he was never intended to bear.

When the man fails to provide the life that is expected of him by the woman, an inevitable breakdown occurs through a disappointment that was always going to happen from an unacceptable expectation.

The man was never built to have that responsibility but the woman must readjust her expectations and return to God as her life source.

In that way, they are both able to bring what they have from the Lord in order to share life together.

We will look further at how the Lord looked after these two and didn't leave them to cope with the results of their actions next.

Chapter 12.

Removed from the garden.

Genesis 3: 17-24
And to the man he said, "Since you listened to your wife and ate from the tree whose fruit I commanded you not to eat, the ground is cursed because of you.

All your life you will struggle to scratch a living from it. It will grow thorns and thistles for you, though you will eat of its grains. By the sweat of your brow will you have food to eat until you return to the ground from which you were made.

For you were made from dust, and to dust you will return."

Then the man—Adam—named his wife Eve, because she would be the mother of all who live.
And the Lord God made clothing from animal skins for Adam and his wife.

Then the Lord God said, "Look, the human beings have become like us, knowing both good and evil. What if they reach out, take fruit from the tree of life, and eat it?

Then they will live forever!" So the Lord God banished them from the Garden of Eden, and he sent Adam out to cultivate the ground from which he had been made.

After sending them out, the Lord God stationed mighty cherubim to the east of the Garden of Eden. And he placed a flaming sword that flashed back and forth to guard the way to the tree of life.

We have looked at what the Lord said to the serpent and Eve.

The Lord turned to Adam next and in response to Adam's claim that *"it was the fault of the woman that the Lord had given him",* made sure that Adam realised that it is he who is responsible for his own actions.

It is very easy to blame others for the way that we respond or behave in any given situation.

Psychologists often place the blame at the feet of irresponsible parents or oppressive siblings.

Sociologists blame the society and circumstances of our surroundings.

The Lord makes it very clear that it is Adam who is to blame for the situation that they find themselves.

Until we learn to appreciate that we are personally responsible for our lives we will never realise that we are in need of a saviour.

Blaming others effectively releases us from any responsibility for our actions which in turn sentences us to an eternal death. - we are never able to repent unless we begin to accept responsibility.

It is because Adam sinned that we live in a fallen world.

It is because we live in rebellion that our own life is out of sync.

It was Adam who was told not to go down that route and it was Adam who listened to the advice of another and disobeyed.

We need to have our ears tuned to the advice of Father and disconnect the ears that listen to the advice of the enemy.

In accepting responsibility the Lord was able to give help and hope for the future.

Had Adam continued with his denial of responsibility the Lord could not have offered any help or hope.

The Lord clearly explained to Adam what his actions would lead to and what he would need to do in order to overcome and live.

Adam is able to prophesy over Eve, giving her a name and declaring that she would be the mother of all living.

In naming Eve Adam took responsibility for her.

He had previously named the birds and animals and been given responsibility for their welfare.

Now he has an added responsibility.

By declaring that she would be the mother of all living they were looking towards the future.

The Lord then clothed them with animal skins.

This is the first time that an animal has been sacrificed and it was done in order to clothe man.

We can see here the first of many signs pointing to the life of Jesus who was sacrificed in order to 'clothe' mankind - Adam's restoration.

Far from being the God of anger and punishment that many have been taught that this incident displays, God clothed them and gave them a hope for the future.

We are now invited into a heavenly conversation between the trinity.

God appreciated the awfulness of their situation - the prospect of living in a fallen world outside of the 'oneness' that they had previously known with God.

"What if the man and woman reach out and take from the tree of life and live forever"?

What a grim prospect that would be for Adam and Eve.

They were now able to make judgments for themselves.

Those judgements will, inevitably, be made from a fallen mindset, susceptible and influenced by the enemy.

Each judgement will lead to further hardship.

The Lord would not want them to have the option of being able to live forever in that state.

He therefore moved them out of the garden - out of the temptation to eat of the tree of life, that He knew they wouldn't be able to resist, and placed mighty cherubim to bar the way.

There was also a flaming sword that flashed backwards and forwards.

Whether the cherubim held the sword or whether it stood alone is unclear.

Cherubim are ministering angels who protect the Lord from assault upon His holiness.

The flaming sword speaks of truth and purity.

The Lord remained in the 'garden'. It is the Lord who is 'the tree of life'.

It wasn't until Jesus opened up the way, for those who come into His kingdom, that the way back into Father's presence was made open again.

We will discover next how Adam and Eve will manage life apart from God.

Chapter 13.

Cain

Genesis 4:1-16
Now Adam had sexual relations with his wife, Eve, and she became pregnant.

When she gave birth to Cain, she said, "With the Lord's help, I have produced a man!"

Later she gave birth to his brother and named him Abel. When they grew up, Abel became a shepherd, while Cain cultivated the ground.

When it was time for the harvest, Cain presented some of his crops as a gift to the Lord .

Abel also brought a gift—the best portions of the firstborn lambs from his flock.

The Lord accepted Abel and his gift, but he did not accept Cain and his gift.

This made Cain very angry, and he looked dejected. "Why are you so angry?" the Lord asked Cain. "Why do you look so dejected? You will be accepted if you do what is right.

But if you refuse to do what is right, then watch out! Sin is crouching at the door, eager to control you.

But you must subdue it and be its master."

One day Cain suggested to his brother, "Let's go out into the fields." And while they were in the field, Cain attacked his brother, Abel, and killed him.

Afterward the Lord asked Cain, "Where is your brother? Where is Abel?" "I don't know," Cain responded. "Am I my brother's guardian?"

But the Lord said, "What have you done? Listen! Your brother's blood cries out to me from the ground! Now you are cursed and banished from the ground, which has swallowed your brother's blood. No longer will the ground yield good crops for you, no matter how hard you work!

From now on you will be a homeless wanderer on the earth."

Cain replied to the Lord, "My punishment is too great for me to bear! You have banished me from the land and from your presence; you have made me a homeless wanderer. Anyone who finds me will kill me!"

The Lord replied, "No, for I will give a sevenfold punishment to anyone who kills you."

Then the Lord put a mark on Cain to warn anyone who might try to kill him.

So Cain left the Lord 's presence and settled in the land of Nod, east of Eden.

There is a lot in the first few chapters of Genesis that is difficult for us to understand when we take more than a brief reading of them.

I have been familiar with Genesis for more than sixty years and there are always more thoughts that unfold as I study it.

I will break with the traditional way of reading here and begin by writing about the end of this section.

In order to get a clearer picture of the scene we need to uncover where it is set.

At the end of this section we read that Cain went out from the presence of the Lord and settled in the land of Nod, east of Eden, with a seal on him that will deter others from killing him.

There are so many 'ifs' and 'buts' to think about in there.

If Cain and Abel are the first children, who are these other people who Cain is concerned about who might want to kill Cain?

If Cain left the 'presence of the Lord' and went to live to the east of Eden, does that mean that Cain and Abel were still living in the garden until that time?

If he is not moving from inside of Eden, why is Eden mentioned?

If they were still living in the garden it might explain how Eve knew about childbirth and also that the events described in Genesis are perhaps not written in sequence.

It may be possible that Adam's family were removed from Eden after this event and not before.

However, if this is so, we will also have to consider whether the sin of Adam in eating of the fruit of the tree of good and evil, that resulted in their removal from the garden, was perhaps not the first sin but a particularly significant and momentous event instead.

Cain's killing of Abel may not have been promoted by sin but ignorance, which will still allow for Adam's sin to be the first and explain why God went to so much trouble to protect him.

For me the story points towards Adam and Eve being taken out of a community of people, who already existed, to be given 'the breath of God', as we who are in God's kingdom, have also been 'born again'.

As we are 'in the world', perhaps Adam and Eve were also 'in the world' but living in harmony; oneness with God; they were 'in the garden' in God's presence.

We must also remember, however, that Eden is given a specific geographical location.

It is also possible that Adam and Eve had other children that we do not know about who Cain was afraid of.

Although it does seem unlikely that he would have had reason to be afraid of them.

These are idle thoughts and of no relevance at all as we were not there and do not have enough evidence of the events to make a judgement.

I simply include them as thoughts that we might want to consider in order to allow Father to break through our previously fast held and rigidly defended understanding.

We have been fed a strict diet of teaching with regards to 'the beginnings' as laid out in the book of Genesis but there is much that is difficult to fit in with that teaching.

There has been a fear in the past that if we begin to think too deeply about what is written we may begin to doubt its authenticity. Or perhaps there was a worry that our faith would fail along with our inability to grasp the realities.

We will be wise to allow the Lord to expand our understanding of His words without failing to appreciate His presence within them.

There is no fear in asking for the words to be rediscovered. The meaning of revelation is having God's words revealed to us.

If scripture does not tally with reality or with itself then we need to find out why or what it is that we are missing.

There is much that is 'assumed' in the story of the creation and the beginnings of mankind, but little known.

If I am building a picture from a jigsaw puzzle and misplace several of the pieces, the scene I am presented with will be severely disjointed.

I must remove and replace all of the pieces that don't fit in order for the picture to become clear.

The book of Genesis often appears to me as a picture that is severely disjointed. I look forward to the clarity that will one day be given.

Historically there has been much teaching of scripture that has been incorrect and misleading.

Often this incorrect teaching has been because there was a need to keep the population in order or to keep them in fear of those in control and more often than not, a misunderstanding of the nature of God.

Teaching from these traditional roots can only be flawed, therefore there is a need for the Lord to renew our minds in order to obtain a fresh revelation of who He is.

Having thought about the possibility that Cain and Abel may or may not have been living in the garden, in the presence of the Lord, we will continue to look at how they developed next.

Chapter 14.

Children - Cain and Abel

Genesis 4:1-16
Now Adam had sexual relations with his wife, Eve, and she became pregnant.

When she gave birth to Cain, she said, "With the Lord 's help, I have produced a man!"

Later she gave birth to his brother and named him Abel. When they grew up, Abel became a shepherd, while Cain cultivated the ground.

When it was time for the harvest, Cain presented some of his crops as a gift to the Lord .

Abel also brought a gift—the best portions of the firstborn lambs from his flock.

The Lord accepted Abel and his gift, but he did not accept Cain and his gift.

This made Cain very angry, and he looked dejected. "Why are you so angry?" the Lord asked Cain. "Why do you look so dejected? You will be accepted if you do what is right.

But if you refuse to do what is right, then watch out! Sin is crouching at the door, eager to control you.

But you must subdue it and be its master."

One day Cain suggested to his brother, "Let's go out into the fields." And while they were in the field, Cain attacked his brother, Abel, and killed him.

Afterward the Lord asked Cain, "Where is your brother? Where is Abel?"

"I don't know," Cain responded. "Am I my brother's guardian?"

But the Lord said, "What have you done? Listen! Your brother's blood cries out to me from the ground!

Now you are cursed and banished from the ground, which has swallowed your brother's blood.

No longer will the ground yield good crops for you, no matter how hard you work!

From now on you will be a homeless wanderer on the earth."

Cain replied to the Lord, "My punishment is too great for me to bear!

You have banished me from the land and from your presence; you have made me a homeless wanderer. Anyone who finds me will kill me!"

The Lord replied, "No, for I will give a sevenfold punishment to anyone who kills you."

Then the Lord put a mark on Cain to warn anyone who might try to kill him.

So Cain left the Lord 's presence and settled in the land of Nod, east of Eden.

Genesis chapter four appears to announce the start of a new era in the life of Adam and Eve.

Eve conceived, bore a child and declared, *"with the Lord's help I have produced a man"*.

Eve acknowledged and is grateful that the Lord has enabled her to have a child, perhaps despite previous events.

She is delighted to have a child and calls him Cain which means, *'gotten from the Lord'*.

Again Eve conceived and bore a second child. She named this one Abel which means, *'passing'*.

Names that are given in scripture often describe character.

Abel's name was very apt. It describes a brief passage of time.

Over some years the Hebrew name which is *'Hevel'*, has come to mean, *'breath'* and describes something that is very brief and apparently meaningless.

These two boys were very different characters as is often the case with first and second siblings.

Cain was full of himself and his ego.

Abel was humble and obedient. Jesus described him as righteous (*Matthew 23:35).*

Cain tilled the ground and grew crops, producing what the ground provided.

Abel became a shepherd and managed flocks.

It is sometimes the case with a first child that the parents are indulgent and allow the child to dictate terms.

Family life can often rotate around a first child and its needs, giving the child a false sense of its own importance.

Whereas a second child tends to fit in with established guides and routines.

The first child will experience new things and the second child will be taken along to them, often waiting until the first child has finished whatever it is they are doing.

In time the two boys brought thank offerings to the Lord.

Abel brought the best of what he had and Cain brought what he had produced from the soil.

The description of Cain's offering is not complementary.

The words, *'Cain brought some of his crops'*, doesn't give the impression that Cain put much effort into his gift or even that it was the 'best of' his crops as Abel's gift was.

The Lord showed His pleasure to Abel and His displeasure in some way to Cain.

Cain became angry.

I get the impression that Cain had a tantrum as spoiled children, and adults, often do when life doesn't go as they might have hoped.

God spoke kindly to Cain and warned him about the danger that he faced if he doesn't learn to overcome his emotions.

"Sin crouches at the door and it will control you".

Perhaps some of us can relate to that statement.

The Lord went on to encourage Cain and told him that he has the ability to control his emotios and he can overcome it.

The Lord gives us the same encouragement throughout the epistles and particularly in the book of Revelation where He gave promises to those who 'overcome' during this life.

There are promises that overcomers will be included to become the bride of Christ and will reign with Him on earth for one thousand years, for example.

I have written about the promises that are awarded to overcomers in my book, 'Some adjustments required'.

We have a greater ability to overcome in our life than Cain had as we have the Spirit of the living God with us.

If the Lord expected Cain to be able to overcome, there is no excuse for us if we fail to do so.

But will Cain learn to overcome?

Chapter 15.

"Sin crouches at the door and it will control you".

Genesis 4:1-16
Now Adam had sexual relations with his wife, Eve, and she became pregnant.

When she gave birth to Cain, she said, "With the Lord's help, I have produced a man!"

Later she gave birth to his brother and named him Abel. When they grew up, Abel became a shepherd, while Cain cultivated the ground.

When it was time for the harvest, Cain presented some of his crops as a gift to the Lord .

Abel also brought a gift—the best portions of the firstborn lambs from his flock.

The Lord accepted Abel and his gift, but he did not accept Cain and his gift.

This made Cain very angry, and he looked dejected. "Why are you so angry?" the Lord asked Cain. "Why do you look so dejected? You will be accepted if you do what is right.

But if you refuse to do what is right, then watch out! Sin is crouching at the door, eager to control you.

But you must subdue it and be its master."

One day Cain suggested to his brother, "Let's go out into the fields." And while they were in the field, Cain attacked his brother, Abel, and killed him.

Afterward the Lord asked Cain, "Where is your brother? Where is Abel?"
"I don't know," Cain responded. "Am I my brother's guardian?"

But the Lord said, "What have you done? Listen! Your brother's blood cries out to me from the ground!
Now you are cursed and banished from the ground, which has swallowed your brother's blood.
No longer will the ground yield good crops for you, no matter how hard you work!

From now on you will be a homeless wanderer on the earth."

Cain replied to the Lord, "My punishment is too great for me to bear!
You have banished me from the land and from your presence; you have made me a homeless wanderer.
Anyone who finds me will kill me!"

The Lord replied, "No, for I will give a sevenfold punishment to anyone who kills you."

Then the Lord put a mark on Cain to warn anyone who might try to kill him.

So Cain left the Lord 's presence and settled in the land of Nod, east of Eden.

The Lord has encouraged Cain to overcome his emotions and warned him what will inevitably happen if he doesn't.

There is a phrase that goes, 'one thing leads to another'. It is a true saying.

'What we sow we will also reap, is another'.

James wrote in his epistle:

Temptation comes from our own desires, which entice us and drag us away. These desires give birth to sinful actions. And when sin is allowed to grow, it gives birth to death.
James 1:14-15 NLT

Jesus also gave a clear warning about the fruit of anger.

"You have heard that our ancestors were told, 'You must not murder. If you commit murder, you are subject to judgment.' But I say, if you are even angry with someone, you are subject to judgment!
Matthew 5:21-22 NLT

It is for this reason that we have been given the power to overcome in the area of our thoughts and emotions.

The battle for how we will spend our eternity begins in our mind and we are given the power and ability to overcome as we work with the Spirit of God towards that end.

Sadly, instead of overcoming his emotions and the thoughts that entered his mind, Cain began to resent his brother Abel - anger turned to resentment and as a result he killed him.

Whilst these thought patterns and emotions had begun during his early years and his parents were responsible, and should have both trained and disciplined him out of them, in his adulthood he became responsible for his own actions.

One day Cain lured Abel to a field and killed him.

Cain decided to attempt to cover up what he had done.

The Lord knew, of course, but asked Cain where his brother was?

Cain replied with a question that revealed both his arrogance and ignorance - the two often live side by side.

"Am I my brother's keeper"?

The question is well known.

And the answer is 'yes, we are our brother's keeper'.

We all exist in order to care for each other.

Our society has become very disconnected. This has a lot to do with the welfare state that has developed during the last one hundred years or so.

We, in the west, tend to believe that 'our brother's' difficulties can be catered for by a state sponsored organisation or perhaps by a charitable organisation.

We have lost a sense of personal responsibility towards our relatives and neighbours. As a consequence society has become fractured; loneliness and poverty abounds.

When it becomes convenient we place our elderly or disabled relatives into a 'home' that can care for them, instead of allowing them to remain amongst those who should have a love and responsibility for them.

But the Lord ignored Cain's question and went to the heart of the matter, destroying Cain's smoke screen of unreality.

As in the situation that Adam and Eve found themselves the Lord explained to Cain the inevitable result of what he had done.

The Lord had already warned Cain of what would happen if he didn't overcome his anger and now he was to bear the fruit of his own failure.

But the Lord said, "What have you done? Listen! Your brother's blood cries out to me from the ground!
Now you are cursed and banished from the ground, which has swallowed your brother's blood.
No longer will the ground yield good crops for you, no matter how hard you work!

From now on you will be a homeless wanderer on the earth"!

Previously the Lord had warned Adam that the ground would be hard and he would have to sweat to make a living.

Now the Lord told Cain that no matter how hard he worked the land would not bear good crops.

There is a correlation between our actions and how 'the ground' responds to us.

We find this principle repeated time and again throughout scripture. We will do well to take notice of this.

Our productivity is dependent upon our ability to overcome the enemy.

Because the ground will no longer produce for Cain he had no choice but to pack up his belongings and find his way elsewhere.

I wonder if Cain had taken responsibility for his actions, repented and overcome his anger whether that judgement might have been reversed?

I suspect so, but the Lord realised that Cain wasn't going to take responsibility, he was still concerned for his own welfare.

Cain was worried that his actions and perhaps his character will encourage others to kill him.

He would be alone and defenseless.

But the Lord was still looking after Cain despite his defiant, arrogant, self pitying attitude.

The Lord placed a mark on Cain to warn anyone who might want to kill him that the Lord would punish them sevenfold.

We are not told what this mark might have been.

So Cain left the presence of the Lord and went to live in the land of Nod which was east of Eden.

Again we get a geographical identification of where the garden of Eden is situated.

The garden of Eden is very much related to the presence of the Lord.

It is where the tree of life and the tree of the knowledge of good and evil are.

These two trees symbolise the life of the Spirit of God and the understanding of wisdom that only flows from God.

We will look at how Cain gets on in his new life next. Will his be a useful life?

Chapter 16.

Cain builds a city.

Genesis 4:17-24
Cain had sexual relations with his wife, and she became pregnant and gave birth to Enoch. Then Cain founded a city, which he named Enoch, after his son.

Enoch had a son named Irad. Irad became the father of Mehujael.
Mehujael became the father of Methushael.
Methushael became the father of Lamech.

Lamech married two women.
The first was named Adah, and the second was Zillah.

Adah gave birth to Jabal, who was the first of those who raise livestock and live in tents.
His brother's name was Jubal, the first of all who play the harp and flute.
Lamech's other wife, Zillah, gave birth to a son named Tubal-cain.
He became an expert in forging tools of bronze and iron.
Tubal-cain had a sister named Naamah.

One day Lamech said to his wives, "Adah and Zillah, hear my voice; listen to me, you wives of Lamech.
I have killed a man who attacked me, a young man who wounded me.

If someone who kills Cain is punished seven times, then the one who kills me will be punished seventy-seven times!"

The peoples on the earth are beginning to expand.

We have here the first detailed list of ancestors and it gives intimate information about Cain's descendents.

Listing descendents - family trees, was an important part of life. It is what explained or characterised who a person was.

This is why we have such a detailed understanding of where various peoples came from, how they relate to each other and where they moved to.

Cain moved east of Eden, found a wife for himself, she gave birth to a son and he founded a city.

We are not given the name of Cain's wife but his son is named Enoch, which means *'to inaugurate or train'*.

Possibly Cain was beginning to see the benefit of training a child well.

It is possible to translate the text as, Cain first had a wife and a son and later moved to Nod.

We may wonder where the wife came from if Adam and Eve were the first people on earth.

Adam and Eve were told to be fruitful and multiply and so it is extremely likely that they would have had many other sons and daughters.

Adam and Eve were created perfectly; there was no defect within their d.n.a. and therefore there would have been no harmful effects from the marriages between close relations.

If there were no other people on the earth at this time, the answer may be that Cain married an elder or younger sibling.

We come across a similarly difficult question later on with the children of Noah.

Cain founded a city and named it after his son - Enoch.

The root of the word that we have for city is 'a fenced off area', or 'stronghold'.

Cain's city probably began as a smallholding with a fence around it to protect the inhabitants from the attacks of wandering tribes and animals.

It is likely to have been built on the top of a high hill.

Despite the mark of protection the Lord placed upon him, Cain is living in fear of his surroundings.

We can see how Cain's character - his ego and self esteem is causing him difficulties.

Adam and his descendants are still living in the shadow of their creator. They had no need of fenced cities because the Lord was their protection and safety.

Cain trusted in his own abilities and he is realising that being away from the Lord is not a good place to be.

We find in scripture that cities generally tend not to be good places to live.

Cities are built and inhabited for the safety of those inside. They are dependent on being enclosed and protected, often by armed warriors, with a high wall or fence.

The inhabitants of cities are not dependent upon the Lord for their safety but on their own abilities.

The people who God uses often live in deserts or open spaces, they herd flocks and live outdoors.

Their dependency for safety is the Lord.

God placed man in 'a garden' but Cain chose to build a city.

In the bible the word city represents government outside of God.

Cain named his city Enoch, after the product of himself.

The city of Enoch became so well known that whenever a fenced area was built afterwards it was called Enoch - city.

When we talk about a city today we can be aware that we are considering a word and concept that originated from Cain's first born.

Cain's city was eventually washed away by the flood in Noah's time but because of its notoriety and strategic position it was later rebuilt and named '*Erech*' which is a variation of the word '*Enoch*'.

Genesis is a book of beginnings and much of what was established in those days remained established, for good or bad.

The city of Erech became a major city, being Nimrod's second capital within the Babylonion empire *(Enoch became Unuk,* then *Uruk and later Erech)* and is still in place today situated in what is now Iraq.

Cain began a people who lived in rebellion towards God.

One of his descendents, Lamech is the first person in scripture to be known to have married two women.

The Lord had given Adam and Eve a structure for family. The bonding of a single man and woman created unity between the two.

Lamech introduced an abnormal deviation from this structure.

It is a structure that denies the bonding of two people and enforces the will of one, over the other two who must inevitably become subordinate to his or her will.

The action of taking a second wife describes a person who is dissatisfied and insecure.

Lamech's first wife was named Adah, and the second was Zillah.

Their children were the first to introduce musical instruments.

This may seem to be a good thing and in some instances it may be but before the fall God had given man a melodic and beautiful voice which no doubt had become tarnished.

We might see the introduction of musical instruments as a substitute for God's creative gift to man or a counterfeit: man's attempt to compensate outside of God's creation.

Another son became proficient in forging iron and bronze.

These too can be made into useful tools but primarily the need is for weapons to kill and destroy.

God had provided all that man needed but there was dissatisfaction and pride in Cain's family.

Lamech killed a man in a fight.

His claim was that he did it in self defence but gives us an indication of how Cain's descendents are not getting on with others too well.

In his fear of a repercussion he declared what he has no right to declare.

He took on the role of God and claimed that "*If someone who kills Cain is punished seven times, then the one who kills me will be punished seventy-seven times!*"

Lamech had no authority to make such a statement, he had not been given authority to judge or condemn another.

Having discovered the way that Cain's family are going we will now return to Adam's other direct descendents - the line that will lead us to Jesus.

Abel is dead - killed by Cain.

Will Adam and Eve bear more children?

Let us find out next.

Chapter 17.

Adams descendents.

Genesis 4:25-26. 5:1-5
Adam had sexual relations with his wife again, and she gave birth to another son.

She named him Seth, for she said, "God has granted me another son in place of Abel, whom Cain killed."
When Seth grew up, he had a son and named him Enosh. At that time people first began to worship the Lord by name.

Chapter 5.
This is the written account of the descendants of Adam.

When God created human beings, he made them to be like himself.

He created them male and female, and he blessed them and called them "human."

When Adam was 130 years old, he became the father of a son who was just like him—in his very image.
He named his son Seth.

After the birth of Seth, Adam lived another 800 years, and he had other sons and daughters.

Adam lived 930 years, and then he died.

Having given us an account of Cain and his descendents we now move back to the line from which Jesus, the redeemer, will come.

Eve gave birth to another son and named him Seth.

The name has its roots in several words and can mean, *'appointed' 'anointed'* or even *'compensated'*.

Eve's words indicate that all of these meanings would be appropriate.

When Seth grew up he had a son and named him Enosh meaning, *'man'*.

Seth was a third son. The third child tends to be more creative and outward looking.

Third children are often pioneers or discoverers and inventors.

This is because the parents are more relaxed and less constrictive upon a third child's activity.

Third children often need to run in order to keep up with older siblings, they gain confidence and life abilities quickly.

Third children are also normally fun children, they laugh easily and amuse others. They tend to be pleasant and easy to get on with as a result of having to find their place in the family.

Eve described Seth as compensation for Abel.

We are told here that after the birth of Seth's son Enosh (not to be confused with Enoch) mankind began to *'call on the Lord by name'*.

This may be a reference to a religious revival and is likely to be a growing awareness, amongst the population, of God.

If we take the writings of Moses as they are written we now have Adam and Eve and their own children but there clearly must be many others in order for the statement to be made.

I am going to stick my neck out and suggest that the influence of Adam's family, who had first hand experience of God, on the other peoples who lived in the land, created a realisation or awareness of God and those others also began to worship Him.

It is inevitable for those who have experienced God first hand that they will reflect that glory to those around them.

We too are called to be life and light to those around us.

The fall of man was a terrible event but the Lord will always bring good out of our mistakes if we work with Him.

The comings and goings of Adam and his family amongst the rest of the population will inevitably release the life that they had flowing through them.

We might imagine that Adam and Eve had thoughts and passions that are similar to ours but we need to remember that thousands of years have passed since the time that they walked with the Lord in the garden.

Adam and Eve were created to live in union with the Lord. Until they were deceived, they were as pure as snow.

Their lives were lived in the presence of God.

If Moses' hair was turned white in the presence of the rear of the Lord, imagine how these people were.

They were a flawed creation but they hadn't had the thousands of years of deterioration that we have experienced.

They may have been 'spoiled goods' but a spoiled Lamborghini is still a better model than a rusty old Ford Cortina.

We might expect a revival or a type of renaissance in the population as those blessings spill out.

Genesis chapter five begins a new era - the descendents of Adam are going to be listed and Moses, the author, likes to recap in order to give us a bit more information.

There are only a couple of lines of recap but there is more to understand.

When God created human beings, he made them to be like himself.

He created them male and female, and he blessed them and called them "human."

The Lord created man with a 'likeness' of Himself.

This may have been in His looks but what does God look like?

Perhaps Adam was a mirror image of Jesus?

But the words speak more about man's morality and character and all that separate us from the animal kingdom.

We live in a fallen world and therefore that image of God in us is also flawed, but Jesus came into the world in order for that image of God in us to be renewed, restored.

The second line may give us another insight into how God created Adam and Eve.

It is perhaps because others were not 'made in the image of God' - they didn't have the breath of God within them, that Moses describes these two as 'human'.

At the beginning of Genesis five we are told that we are going to be given an account of the descendents of Adam but, perhaps unsurprisingly, there is no account of either Cain or Abel in there.

They have been omitted as if they never were.

Moses begins the account with Seth.

We might have expected a mention of righteous Abel with the word 'deceased' in brackets after his name or of Cain, the first born, with the words 'departed from the Lord' or some such comment.

But, for Moses, the old has gone and the new has come.

Seth was a man who was the exact image of Adam.

This may also refer to his looks but is more likely a reference to his character and might explain why there was an awakening during the time of his son.

Adam lived for 930 years.

I will be coming back to the ages of these individuals, but that will be a reading for another day.

Chapter 18.

From Seth to Noah

Genesis 5:6-32
When Seth was 105 years old, he became the father of
Enosh.
After the birth of Enosh, Seth lived another 807 years,
and he had other sons and daughters.

Seth lived 912 years, and then he died.

When Enosh was 90 years old, he became the father of
Kenan.

After the birth of Kenan, Enosh lived another 815 years,
and he had other sons and daughters.
Enosh lived 905 years, and then he died.
When Kenan was 70 years old, he became the father of
Mahalalel.

After the birth of Mahalalel, Kenan lived another 840
years, and he had other sons and daughters.
Kenan lived 910 years, and then he died.
When Mahalalel was 65 years old, he became the father
of Jared.
After the birth of Jared, Mahalalel lived another 830
years, and he had other sons and daughters.

Mahalalel lived 895 years, and then he died.

When Jared was 162 years old, he became the father of Enoch.

After the birth of Enoch, Jared lived another 800 years, and he had other sons and daughters.

Jared lived 962 years, and then he died.

When Enoch was 65 years old, he became the father of Methuselah.

After the birth of Methuselah, Enoch lived in close fellowship with God for another 300 years, and he had other sons and daughters.

Enoch lived 365 years, walking in close fellowship with God. Then one day he disappeared, because God took him.

When Methuselah was 187 years old, he became the father of Lamech.

After the birth of Lamech, Methuselah lived another 782 years, and he had other sons and daughters.

Methuselah lived 969 years, and then he died.

When Lamech was 182 years old, he became the father of a son.

Lamech named his son Noah, for he said, "May he bring us relief from our work and the painful labor of farming this ground that the Lord has cursed."

After the birth of Noah, Lamech lived another 595 years, and he had other sons and daughters.
Lamech lived 777 years, and then he died.

After Noah was 500 years old, he became the father of Shem, Ham, and Japheth.

The start of the line of Adam.

We will begin with some interesting facts:

I will give the numbers in numerals rather than words as I believe it will be easier for the reader to get a picture of scale.

There are some 1,646 years from Adam until Noah is born.

All of the people listed above, with the exception of Noah, were alive during the life of both Adam and his son Seth.

We can be sure that both Adam and Seth taught each following generation about the events that had passed previously.

Everyone except Noah and his family, were born before Adam died.

None of the people died until after Adam died.

Adam's life spanned the births of all who are mentioned on the list.

In scripture, Adam is the first born and also the first who died, with the exception of Abel who was murdered by Cain.

We can see that it was the fruit of Adam's sin that caused the death of Abel and also brought about his own death.

Methuselah died in the same year as the flood.

Methuselah's son, Lamech, died five years before the flood.

Whilst Adam was alive, eight generations were born but after his death each generation died with the exception of Noah, who began a new era.

Enosh, Kenan, Mahalalel, Jared, Methuselah and Lamech were all alive at the same time as Noah.

Noah's children knew Methuselah for one hundred years.

Noah was 600 years old when Methuselah died at the age of 969.

Everyone on the list, except Seth, knew both Noah and Adam.

With the noticeable exception of Enoch, who we will talk about next time.

Noah had some knowledgeable teachers and so when we read about the events that occurred from the beginning we can know that Noah had knowledge from those who had a first hand experience of them.

It is not the case that stories that were handed down had become twisted or distorted.

We read that all of the people listed had other unnamed sons and daughters who presumably were contemporaries of Noah and yet we make the assumption that Noah built the ark and collected the animals etc. alone.

Or perhaps that was only my assumption.

Although they aren't named, there were, perhaps, many family members available to help.

Noah alone was righteous but that doesn't necessarily mean that others were not there to assist in his vision - in his obedience.

The longevity of these people appears extraordinary to us who live comparatively short lives but for Adam and Eve who had no thought of ever dying, until sin became a part of them, their lives must have flown past quickly.

The following generations too, who had not experienced their forebears dying until Adam did, would have thought nothing of living to a long age, although death would have been expected eventually.

The oldest person to have lived was Methuselah who didn't quite reach 1000 years and died at the age of 969.

So how do we explain this long life?

We read that at the time of the flood the Lord opened the heavens to allow the waters that had been held above *(Gen. 1:6-8)* to be released. *Gen. 7:11-8:2.*

After the flood we read that the life span expectancy rapidly decreased to a similar period that we experience today.

It is likely then that the waters that had been held in the sky until the time of the flood had screened the population from the harmful effects of the sun enabling a longer life span.

It is also probable that sin has become a debilitating factor, increasing illnesses and the effects that the continued assaults on our bodies by the enemy have, in reducing both our mental expectancy (what we believe and speak is what becomes our reality) and the physical strain of living in a fallen world.

The life span of Lamech, Noah's dad, (not to be confused with Cain's rebellious offspring who was also called Lamech), tells us something of his character.

Lamech has the shortest life and clocks up seven hundred and seventy seven years.

In scripture the number seven is the number of completeness.

Lamech is the last father before Noah and it is his life that completes the era that ends with Noah.

The fruit of Lamech's life was the righteous life of Noah.

We know that good fruit can only grow from a good tree and so we can also understand that Lamech served the Lord diligently.

I have always assumed, and I believe correctly, that the line of Seth is a line of righteous people, otherwise why would these particular people be on that list rather than others?

We see in scripture a parallel between the unrighteous line of Cain, who killed his brother, and the righteous line of Seth.

Seth is cited as being a righteous man.

We are told with regards to Enoch that 'he walked with God'.

At the birth of Noah, Lamech was able to prophesy over him.

Lamech named his son Noah, for he said, "May he bring us relief from our work and the painful labor of farming this ground that the Lord has cursed."
Genesis 5:29 NLT

We know that Lamech's prophecy was spot on, and not simply an exasperated father's wish, because after the flood we find that Noah built an altar and made a sacrifice to the Lord.
The Lord was pleased with the aroma of the sacrifice and said to himself, "I will never again curse the ground because of the human race.
Genesis 8:21 NLT

Methuselah, whose name means, *'his death will bring judgement'*, was named by his father, Enoch, in anticipation of an end to the suffering that they were experiencing.

Methuselah died in the same year as the flood.

As promised at the beginning, we have arrived at the life of Enoch now and we will look at his story next.

Adam's family tree:

0.   Adam.

            Abel is murdered.
            Cain moved away from the Lord.

130.   Seth Born.

235.   Enosh Born.

315.   Kenan Born.

385.   Mahalalel Born.

450.   Jared Born.

612.   Enoch Born.

677.   Methuselah Born.

930.   Adam Died. age 930.

977.   Enoch was not found at age 365.

1042.   Seth Died. age 912.

1046.   Noah Born.

1130 or 1140. Enosh Died. age 905.

1225.	Kenan Died. age 910.
1280.	Mahalalel Died. age 895.
1412.	Jared Died. age 962.
1546.	Shem, Ham and Japheth Born. (triplets)?
1641.	Lamech Died. age 777.
1646.	Methuselah Died. age 969.
1646.	The flood begins.
1647.	The flood subdues.

Chapter 19.

Enoch.

Genesis 5:18-24
When Jared was 162 years old, he became the father of
Enoch.

After the birth of Enoch, Jared lived another 800 years,
and he had other sons and daughters.

Jared lived 962 years, and then he died.

When Enoch was 65 years old, he became the father of
Methuselah.

After the birth of Methuselah, Enoch lived in close
fellowship with God for another 300 years, and he had
other sons and daughters.

Enoch lived 365 years, walking in close fellowship with
God. Then one day he disappeared, because God took
him.

I have left the life of Enoch until last, in looking at the list of Adam's descendents, because he stands out in a particular way.

All the information we have with regards to Enoch is a couple of small sentences.

'Enoch lived 365 years, walking in close fellowship with God. Then one day he disappeared, because God took him'. Genesis 5: 22-24

We must take some time to analyze what we know of his life and passing because what we believe of Enoch will affect our understanding of heaven, eternal life, the kingdom of God, and our foundation of faith.

The writer to the Hebrews, when talking about people of faith, tells us that.
'It was by faith that Enoch was taken up to heaven without dying—"he disappeared, because God took him." For before he was taken up, he was known as a person who pleased God'.
Hebrews 11:5 NLT

The same writer to the Hebrews uses a similar idea when describing king Melchizedec, who met Abraham after a mighty battle.

Because there are no details of Mechizedek's birth or death in scripture, the writer uses Melchizedek in a symbolic way, as a man who 'lived forever'. *Hebrews. 7:13-17.*

In a similar manner the writer to the Hebrews takes the same verse that we have in Genesis, with regards to Enoch 'not being found', and expands it to make Enoch an example of the reward for 'living in faith' and declares that *'he was taken to heaven'.*

The writer's declaration is not found elsewhere in scripture however.

We know from our verse in Genesis 5 that Enoch was a righteous man and he walked with God.

The only other thing that we know for sure is that *'he couldn't be found'.*

We are told that *'God took him'.*

The fact that Enoch 'disappeared and couldn't be found' implies that people were looking for him.

There is another incident where a person was taken up into the sky and couldn't be found, although many people looked for him.

This was when Elijah, who was a great and notable prophet, was taken up into the sky by a fiery chariot at the end of his ministry. *2. Kings. 2:11.*

He had just handed over his cloak to Elisha, who was to come after him, and all those around saw him taken away in this manner.

Elisha told the people around not to go looking for him, but they did anyway, in case he had been dropped on a nearby mountain, but they couldn't find him.

The prophets, who were his students, clearly had no thought that he had been taken to heaven.

It has often been assumed that he too was taken into 'heaven' but when we study scripture further we find that ten years after this incident, in a final work of his ministry, he wrote a letter to king Jehoram. *2 Chronicles 21:12.*

It is doubtful that Elijah wrote the letter from heaven, but that he was still alive. God had taken him to a place where Elisha, who came after him, would not be overshadowed by the presence of his predecessor.

The death of Moses is another incident that involved a supernatural burial, similar to that of Enoch's.

Moses misrepresented God when leading the Israelites through the desert and as a consequence, although he was a man who 'walked with God', he was not allowed to enter the land that the Israelites inherited but was allowed to stand on the top of a mountain to view it from outside.

Afterwards God 'took him' and buried him on Mount Nebo.

There were no humans at the burial of Moses.

The place was kept secret, presumably because God didn't want his place of death to become a shrine, as had the cave of Machpelah where Abraham and his family were buried and the tomb where Rachael, Jacob's wife, was buried.

There has never been another prophet in Israel like Moses, whom the Lord knew face to face.
Deuteronomy 34:10 NLT

Both of these men walked with God, as we have heard that Enoch did, and after they were *'taken away by God'*, they were *'not to be found'*.

Only God and the angels knew where they were.

We have no knowledge of the burial of either Moses or Elijah. In the same way as the passing of Enoch, they were not to be found because God took them.

Enoch was a righteous man who walked with God.

His life span was extremely short in comparison to those who went before and came after, just 365 years that we know of.

If he was 'taken into heaven', I will not argue the point but scripture doesn't tell us that.

The manner of his early departure may be noteworthy but we are not given any details. If he was a righteous man, an example to others on earth, why would God remove him?

It is possible, and even likely, that his place of burial was concealed as Moses was by God.

I have heard many preachers talk about the fact that there are two men in heaven as well as Jesus - Elijah and Enoch.

Whilst this might be the case, I don't see any reason why they would be with God in that way, and I have found no evidence in scripture to support that they are and much evidence to suggest that they are not.

There have been many who have been raised from the dead only to die again, but in truth Paul made it very clear that there are none besides Jesus who have been raised to eternity.

He wrote to the Corinthians about this very issue:

But in fact, Christ has been raised from the dead. He is the first of a great harvest of all who have died.

But there is an order to this resurrection: Christ was raised as the first of the harvest; then all who belong to Christ will be raised when he comes back.
1 Corinthians 15:20, 23 NLT

If Christ was the first fruit, how can there be others who have gone before?

What we understand of heaven has an impact on what expectations we have with regards to the return of Jesus to reign on earth.

There are many today who believe that heaven is a place that we go to when we die.

Some of that reasoning is based upon a belief that there are already people inhabiting a place called heaven.

When Peter addressed the crowds at the time of Pentecost he made it clear that David had never ascended to heaven. *Acts 2:34.*

Paul also made it clear in his letter to Timothy that the resurrection of the dead has not yet occurred and is yet to happen.
They have left the path of truth, claiming that the resurrection of the dead has already occurred; in this way, they have turned some people away from the faith.
2 Timothy 2:18 NLT

In the light of this we can be sure that heaven is not a place that is filled with people who have died - the resurrection has not yet occurred.

The only person who is definitely in heaven with Jesus is the thief who died on the cross next to Jesus.

Or is he?

Then he said, "Jesus, remember me when you come into your Kingdom."
And Jesus replied, "I assure you, today you will be with me in paradise."
Luke 23:42-43 NLT

Despite what the preachers have historically taught us, when we look at the scripture, we find that the thief didn't ask Jesus if he could 'go to heaven'.

The thief was aware of the teaching of Jesus - that He would be coming back to earth to reign, and asked instead, to be remembered when Jesus came *'back to His kingdom'*.

The translators, who have placed the punctuation in this text, have, I believe, placed a comma in the wrong place in Jesus' answer, as otherwise the reply of Jesus doesn't make sense and Jesus doesn't answer the thief's question.

When we move the comma one word to the right we will see that Jesus answered the thief's question.

And Jesus replied, "I assure you today, you will be with me in paradise."

This is the problem with the translators placing their own understanding of scripture over the more likely translation.

Why would Jesus have given the thief an answer that he hadn't asked a question to?

We know too that Jesus wouldn't have lied to the thief to tell him that he would be with Him on that day, as Jesus wasn't at home on that day, He was still in the grave.

Jesus answered the thief's question by assuring him solemnly that he would be with Jesus when Jesus returned to His kingdom on earth.

We can come to the conclusion that the only person who we can be sure is in 'heaven' with God is Jesus, who is God.

The question we might like to think about then is, where or what is heaven?

Heaven is the place where God dwells.

God dwells among His people.

We are His temple.

Jesus said that, *"The kingdom of God is within you".*
Luke 17:21

God is Spirit and not human and therefore does not need a physical place to dwell but covers Himself in His own glory.

Heaven has been compared to the clouds.

When the Israelites were tramping through the desert the presence of God travelled with them as 'a cloud' by day and a fire by night.

When Jesus went back 'to heaven' after His resurrection He was seen to disappear into 'the clouds'.

When Jesus returns to reign on earth He will be coming back in 'the clouds' i.e. coming out of heaven, or to put it another way, He will be bringing heaven with Him.

We are called to be a people who 'dwell in the presence of God'. God is our 'dwelling place'.

To put all of that together then.

If we dwell in the presence of God, and heaven is also where God is, does that mean that we are a people who dwell in heaven?

God dwells amongst His people and Jesus said that, *"The kingdom of God is within you". Luke 17:21*

If this is so, when Jesus returns to reign, might He be returning from out of the people who dwell with God in heaven?

Is this why we need to grow into maturity so that Jesus is able to return, through us, and will be seen on the earth through His people?

There is a need for us to become a people who stop being temporary visitors but to dwell permanently in heaven - in the presence of God, to enable Jesus to return on earth.

If we believe that heaven is a geographical or physical place, we will always be waiting until we die to enter a place that we are born to live in now.

The curse that the first man brought upon creation has been lifted.

We, along with all of creation, are redeemed.

We can now enter and live in 'the holy place' - heaven, because Jesus came, suffered, died and rose again in order to redeem us from that curse in full.

Let us hasten the return of Jesus, seek to dwell permanently in that place of redemption, so that Jesus might be reflected in us.

At this time, in our own history we are entering a new era - God's kingdom era.

Let's look next at the world that Noah was entering.

Chapter 20.

A fallen world.

Genesis 6:1-8
Then the people began to multiply on the earth, and daughters were born to them.
The sons of God saw the beautiful women and took any they wanted as their wives.

Then the Lord said, "My Spirit will not put up with humans for such a long time, for they are only mortal flesh. In the future, their normal lifespan will be no more than 120 years."

In those days, and for some time after, giant Nephilites lived on the earth, for whenever the sons of God had intercourse with women, they gave birth to children who became the heroes and famous warriors of ancient times.

The Lord observed the extent of human wickedness on the earth, and he saw that everything they thought or imagined was consistently and totally evil.

So the Lord was sorry he had ever made them and put them on the earth.

It broke his heart. And the Lord said, "I will wipe this human race I have created from the face of the earth. Yes, and I will destroy every living thing—all the people, the large animals, the small animals that scurry along the ground, and even the birds of the sky. I am sorry I ever made them."

But Noah found favor with the Lord .

There has been much written about and even more assumed and discussed with regards to this passage.

There are various well thought out theories both biblical and unbiblical, some of which include aliens from space, which we won't go into.

No conclusions have yet been reached by biblical scholars, who have studied scripture in detail over many years.

But despite the mountain of research and years of study that has been carried out by knowledgeable, well qualified and very experienced scholars, I will attempt here to give a very brief outline.

Please feel free to carry out your own research into this passage. It will be good practice and you will find it interesting.

Most of the debate relates around the fact that Moses, the author of Genesis, calls this line of beings - the Nephilim, *'the sons of God'*.

Can fallen angels be called 'the sons of God'?

The book of Enoch, which is not in the bible and therefore does not come under the cloak of 'being inspired by God', calls them 'the sons of heaven'.

The main theories are that these 'sons of God' are: Fallen angels, fallen children of the sons of Seth, fallen children from the line of Cain or fallen men from either line who have been overtaken by fallen angels.

I have personally, at a stroke, discarded the latter three theories on the basis that the Nephilim are described as 'giants'.

Had the initiators of the line of the Nephilim been men, why would the offspring become 'men of renown' or 'giants' as the king James version has it, and as the Israelites describe them later?

The Nephilim are also mentioned as inhabiting Canaan, after the flood and at the time of the Exodus.

They are called 'sons of Anak'. Anak appears to have been a leader.

It is also believed that Goliath who fought, unsuccessfully, against the Israelites was a descendant of these giants.

If our assumptions are correct, that the Nephilim were the result of fallen angels who mated with human females and that the tribe of Anak were descended from this unholy alliance, we must also assume that there were members of that tribe who merged with those around them, as Goliath and his family certainly did at Gath after they were evicted from Canaan.

In which case we can also assume that their D.N.A. may also have been passed down to following generations to this day.

A fact which may account for the occasional occurrence of unusually tall people who exist today.

Did these descendents survive the great flood? Were they able to swim? Or are they another group of people who have been produced by fallen angels after the flood?

We can read in verse four that Moses writes, *'In those days, and for some time after, giant Nephilites lived on the earth, for whenever the sons of God had intercourse with women, they gave birth to children who became the heroes and famous warriors of ancient times.*

Moses will have known of the Nephilim in Canaan and we can assume, but not know for sure, that he was referring to these in his, *'sometime after'.*

But there does remain a slight problem with the initiators being fallen angels, in that nowhere in scripture do we find that spiritual beings, fallen or not, are able to produce offspring.

The only exception being when the Spirit of God and a lady named Mary produced a boy called Jesus.

It may be that fallen angels, who are able to manifest themselves in various forms, were able to produce offspring when mating with human beings.

The book of Enoch:

And the angels, the children of the heaven, saw and lusted after them, and said to one another: 'Come, let us choose us wives from among the children of men and beget us children.' And Semjaza, who was their leader, said unto them: 'I fear ye will not indeed agree to do this deed, and I alone shall have to pay the penalty of a great sin.' And they all answered him and said: 'Let us all swear an oath, and all bind ourselves by mutual imprecations not to abandon this plan but to do this thing.' Then sware they all together and bound themselves by mutual imprecations upon it. And they were in all two hundred; who descended in the days of Jared on the summit of Mount Hermon, and they called it Mount Hermon, because they had sworn and bound themselves by mutual imprecations upon it.

Whether or not the book of Enoch is inspired by God, this text does reveal to us that the people of that period believed that the children of God, or 'heaven' were fallen angels.

The Lord looked at the scene on earth and saw that everywhere was turmoil, sin and violence.

How He must have sorrowed at what had become of His creation.

The Lord said that He will not always put up with man for such a long time.

As we discussed in a previous chapter, man had long life spans.

This word from the Lord confirms for me that the life spans given previously were the actual periods that each individual lived rather than it being the time span of a tribe of people or a generation with that name, as some have suggested.

The Lord has decided that a life span of almost one thousand years is too long.

We must bear in mind that the intention for man was not one thousand years, but eternity.

The Lord has spent some sixteen hundred years showing us good reason why a shorter life span would be better for us, given our propensity for evil.

The Lord declared that one hundred and twenty years is time enough for man and from the time of the flood the expectancy of life began to reduce.

The life of Moses spanned exactly one hundred and twenty years.

The Nephilim, or Nephilites are described by Moses as being *'the heroes and warriors of ancient times'*.

We know today about the stories from Greek mythology of mighty men and gods who carried out various deeds on earth.

It is quite likely that it was the Nephilim who the Greeks were referring to in those half remembered and disjointed stories that were retold from generation to generation.

The Babylonion and other nations will have rewritten and elaborated on the truth of the situation on earth as they did with the epic poems of Gilgamesh, within which are many stories that correspond with the book of Genesis, disjointed and corrupt as they are.

We may wonder why, or how, it was that fallen angels during those days appeared as mighty warriors or as giants when, although spiritual beings live for eternity, we don't see these creatures today.

My own thinking on this is that these fallen creatures were originally created by God to be splendid and wondrous beings.

No doubt during these early days, even though they had rebelled and been 'cast down to earth', they might still retain some of those glorious features although marred and twisted.

Today we do not see them perhaps because their form has become so unpleasant and evil, due to the perpetual state of sin that they inhabit, that to show themselves would be to alert mankind to the deception that they wish to be kept secret.

Perhaps too they have lost the ability to become visible along with other attributes that they were originally given.

However, we do know that they still inhabit the minds and thoughts of all who wish to submit to the enemy, who is satan.

Moses wrote of the Lord that It *'broke his heart'*.
And the Lord said, "I will wipe this human race I have created from the face of the earth. Yes, and I will destroy every living thing—all the people, the large animals, the small animals that scurry along the ground, and even the birds of the sky. I am sorry I ever made them."

Notice that Moses is still concerned with *'the small animals that scurry along the ground'*.

But Noah found favor with the Lord.

The Lord has made a covenant with man, that through the woman, one day, will come a redeemer.

There must be a remnant who survives. The Lord, as always, has a plan.

The Lord's plan is held in a man called Noah.

Chapter 21.

Noah.

Genesis 6:9-22.
This is the account of Noah and his family.
Noah was a righteous man, the only blameless person living on earth at the time, and he walked in close fellowship with God.

Noah was the father of three sons: Shem, Ham, and Japheth.
Now God saw that the earth had become corrupt and was filled with violence.
God observed all this corruption in the world, for everyone on earth was corrupt.

So God said to Noah, "I have decided to destroy all living creatures, for they have filled the earth with violence.
Yes, I will wipe them all out along with the earth!

"Build a large boat from cypress wood and waterproof it with tar, inside and out. Then construct decks and stalls throughout its interior. Make the boat 450 feet long, 75 feet wide, and 45 feet high. Leave an 18-inch opening below the roof all the way around the boat.
Put the door on the side, and build three decks inside the boat—lower, middle, and upper.

"Look! I am about to cover the earth with a flood that will destroy every living thing that breathes.
Everything on earth will die.

But I will confirm my covenant with you.

So enter the boat—you and your wife and your sons and their wives.
Bring a pair of every kind of animal—a male and a female—into the boat with you to keep them alive during the flood. of every kind of bird, and every kind of animal, and every kind of small animal that scurries along the ground, will come to you to be kept alive.

And be sure to take on board enough food for your family and for all the animals."

So Noah did everything exactly as God had commanded him.

The name Noah means *'relief'* or *'comfort'*.

Lamech, Noah's father, named him with a prophecy that he would bring relief from the hard work caused by the curse that had been placed on the land through the sin of Adam.

Moses is keen to emphasise the wickedness and violence that reigned on earth at that time and cites the obedience of Noah in opposition to all that surrounded him.

We must be careful when we read the words of Moses that we don't leave Noah in isolation, a lone soul who lived for five hundred years of his life with no companions.

Noah alone stood head and shoulders above his peers in terms of righteousness as is evidenced by his obedience in hearing God.

But in claiming that everyone else was evil, are we including his father, Lamech amongst that number? Or Methuselah, his grandfather? Or his wife and children, Shem, Ham and Japheth?

We read that Lamech had other sons and daughters besides Noah. Were they all wicked people?

Is Moses talking about a period immediately before the flood when perhaps all of his direct relatives had passed away?

We know that Methuselah was spared death until the same year as the flood and Noah's father died just five years previously.

Noah was certainly the only person who lived in obedience, hearing what the Lord was saying and putting his faith in the words of the Lord into action.

Noah was born into an era that was coming to an end.

Jesus spoke about the times of Noah:

"When the Son of Man returns, it will be like it was in Noah's day.
In those days before the flood, the people were enjoying banquets and parties and weddings right up to the time Noah entered his boat.
People didn't realize what was going to happen until the flood came and swept them all away. That is the way it will be when the Son of Man comes.
Matthew 24:37-39 NLT

Jesus isn't saying that when He returns to reign on earth, the people will be swept away in a flood or some other disaster.

He is pointing out that, in the same way as the people in Noah's day, those who don't know Him, won't be aware of the times that they are living in.

Today, we too are living in similar times. We are at the end of one era - the church era.

We are entering a new era - God's kingdom age.

Many, including God's children, are unaware of the times that we are living in.

If we are aware and want to journey through into God's kingdom age, God has prepared an ark, as He did in Noah's day.

The ark that God has prepared in these times isn't made of wood and sealed with tar as Noah's was but is made of people living in fellowship with other people.

The planks of wood are not sealed with tar to ensure that they are watertight but the relationships are sealed with love to keep them bonded.

Many will cling on to the temporary rituals and tradition of the old wine skin that they have lived with for two thousand years to keep themselves afloat, but the new wine skin is not built from the old, but is completely new.

The old can not contain the new wine that is being poured out at this time.

God gave Noah specific instructions as to how he must build the ark.

Had Noah not listened or decided that he knew a better way, he would not have travelled through to the new day that was coming.

God was very precise about the measurements and construction of the ark, even to the detail of leaving an 18" opening below the roof all the way around.

Can we imagine the intensity of the fumes inside had that opening not been there?

Because of the wickedness that prevailed on earth God told Noah that He will destroy all living things, people, animals, birds and small animals *'that scurry along the ground'*.

Nothing will live.

Noah might have believed that he too would be included in that number but the Lord gave him an assurance.
"But I will confirm my covenant with you".

God's covenant had originally been given to Eve, in that a redeemer would be given. It will be interesting to find out whether God's covenant to Noah will be the same.

This initial instruction to Noah appears to be a broad outline, something to get him started perhaps.

Noah was given the size of the ark and told to collect pairs of animals and plenty of food for himself, his family, the birds and the animals.

The Lord told Noah that the animals would come to him.

"every kind of bird, and every kind of animal, and every kind of small animal that scurries along the ground, will come to you to be kept alive".

Later we find that the Lord expanded the numbers of pairs of some animals to seven, those used for eating and sacrifice, and the number of pairs of birds to seven also so that they might breed.

It has been my own experience that the Lord gives information in stages.

Very often we are told to go somewhere or to meet someone or to do something and it is not until we have obeyed that instruction that we are given more information about the purpose and how to accomplish that purpose.

When I began work I had very little knowledge of the work that I felt the Lord had asked me to embark on but I discovered that I was able to accept any work that I was asked to do because with each job I was given the

Lord also gave me the understanding of how to accomplish it.

This way of working not only built up my knowledge of the trades that I was able to be competent in but, of far greater importance, is that it built a faith in the Lord and a knowledge that He would never give me anything to do that He wouldn't help me to accomplish.

Having worked in that way for most of my life it has been fairly straightforward to be able to transfer the same principle to other issues in life.

There are no mountains that we cannot climb if we acknowledge the Lord, appreciate that nothing comes into our lives that He hasn't allowed, and are willing to work with Him in order to overcome.

I am sure that Noah too experienced at first hand the voice of God explaining which types of joints to make at each intersection of timber, where to get the best timber from and what size nails to use etc.

There must have been a mountain of information to be learnt about animal welfare also as well as administration skills and cage requirements.

Which animals could be left alone with each other without being eaten for example.

We will discover if Noah has been listening correctly next.

Will his boat and cargo sink to the depths?

Chapter 22.

The flood waters.

Genesis 7:1-24.
When everything was ready, the Lord said to Noah, "Go into the boat with all your family, for among all the people of the earth, I can see that you alone are righteous.

Take with you seven pairs—male and female—of each animal I have approved for eating and for sacrifice, and take one pair of each of the others.
Also take seven pairs of every kind of bird.

There must be a male and a female in each pair to ensure that all life will survive on the earth after the flood.

Seven days from now I will make the rains pour down on the earth.
And it will rain for forty days and forty nights, until I have wiped from the earth all the living things I have created."

So Noah did everything as the Lord commanded him.

Noah was 600 years old when the flood covered the earth.
He went on board the boat to escape the flood—he and his wife and his sons and their wives.

With them were all the various kinds of animals—those approved for eating and for sacrifice and those that were not—along with all the birds and the small animals that scurry along the ground.

They entered the boat in pairs, male and female, just as God had commanded Noah.

After seven days, the waters of the flood came and covered the earth.
When Noah was 600 years old, on the seventeenth day of the second month, all the underground waters erupted from the earth, and the rain fell in mighty torrents from the sky.

The rain continued to fall for forty days and forty nights.
That very day Noah had gone into the boat with his wife and his sons—Shem, Ham, and Japheth—and their wives.
With them in the boat were pairs of every kind of animal—domestic and wild, large and small—along with birds of every kind.

Two by two they came into the boat, representing every living thing that breathes.
A male and female of each kind entered, just as God had commanded Noah.

Then the Lord closed the door behind them.

For forty days the floodwaters grew deeper, covering the ground and lifting the boat high above the earth.

As the waters rose higher and higher above the ground, the boat floated safely on the surface.
Finally, the water covered even the highest mountains on the earth, rising more than twenty-two feet above the highest peaks.
All the living things on earth died—birds, domestic animals, wild animals, small animals that scurry along the ground, and all the people.
Everything that breathed and lived on dry land died.

God wiped out every living thing on the earth—people, livestock, small animals that scurry along the ground, and the birds of the sky.

All were destroyed.

The only people who survived were Noah and those with him in the boat.
And the floodwaters covered the earth for 150 days.

The Lord's instructions to Noah, as outlined by Moses, are very specific and repetitious.

I wonder if the Lord had to repeat Himself several times to Noah or if He had to repeat Himself to Moses or if Moses wrote it down in a repetitive manner as an aid for readers to remember it?

Moses gives some information, that appears to be from the mouth of the Lord, that we might have thought is unnecessary given the close proximity that early man experienced with the animal kingdom.

There must be a male and a female in each pair to ensure that all life will survive on the earth after the flood.

There are some today who will disagree with Moses.

Noah is also told how long the rain will last for, so that he can prepare accordingly.

The rain will last for forty days and forty nights.

The number forty in scripture is one to be noted.

Jesus spent forty days fasting.

There were forty days from the time of Jesus' resurrection until His ascension.

Moses' life was split into three periods of forty.

He also spent forty days on Mount Sinai.

Jonah warned Nineveh for forty days with regards to their sins.

There are many other examples.

The number forty appears to be a period of testing but can also symbolise a generation.

Noah was six hundred years old when he went into the ark.

The Lord waited until everything was ready and then told Noah that in seven days, the number of completion, the rains would commence.

On the seventh day the heavens were opened and the waters that were under the ground were set free and bubbled up.

There is some discussion as to whether this is the first occasion that it rained.

In our first chapters we learned that the plants were watered by springs that bubbled up from beneath the ground.

If this is the first instance of rain it may well account for why the earth was so hard for them to manage.

Moses makes the point that the rain started on the very day that Noah went into the ark.

I wonder if those around saw the rain falling as a strange coincidence?

The Lord closed the door after Noah had entered as if He was shutting the lid on a people who had ignored Him.

There was now no escape from the judgement that is to come.

The waters rose, taking the ark with it until the tops of the mountains were covered and everything that lived had been swept away.

'Everything that breathed and lived on dry land died'.

The waters rose for forty days but the flood waters covered the earth for one hundred and fifty days.

That is approximately five months.

Will they be able to leave the ark after five months?

I have noticed that Moses has mentioned *'the small animals that scurry along the ground'*, no less than three times in this section.

Noah and family have a long period in the ark ahead of them.

The ark seems to be watertight and is holding up.

So far so good.

Chapter 23.

As it was in the days of Noah.

Genesis chapters 1-8.
We are moving out of the first era of creation.

We have seen the righteous line of Adam, beginning with Seth living in parallel with the unrighteous line of Cain who were going from bad to worse.

In each generation God looked for a man who was faithful and He was not disappointed.

God had a plan for His covenant with man to be completed and despite what appeared to be happening on the ground, He was pursuing that plan.

We live in similar times, as the world becomes more rebellious and defiant towards a loving God.

Noah was born into a time of change, his life spanned two of earth's eras.

We too are living in a period where the old era is departing as we journey into the era of God's kingdom age.

The world is being shaken at this time in preparation for change.

Noah was born into a time of rebellion on earth.

The Lord saw that rebellion towards God had reached a climax. He could stand no more.

Noah is described as a man of righteousness because he was obedient.

He was given one hundred years to build the ark that the Lord described to him whilst the world looked on and ignored the opportunity they had to change their ways.

Whether we believe Noah's story or not is largely immaterial. It is written for our benefit to teach us something of the plans of the Lord.

There are records of a great flood that occurred within the writings of most cultures that existed after that time.

Scientists and archaeologists are now also coming around to the idea that such a flood did occur, was caused by a meteor storm and that the receding flood waters are now situated frozen at the north and south poles.

We can see that probability evidenced by the fear of climate overheating and expectation that if the poles are to eventually melt the world will be enveloped by water.

We can be sure that this won't happen however, as the Lord has promised that it won't.

Yes, I am confirming my covenant with you. Never again will floodwaters kill all living creatures; never again will a flood destroy the earth".
Genesis 9:11 NLT

Jesus will be returning to reign on earth as He has said that He would.

Then everyone will see the Son of Man coming on the clouds with great power and glory.
Mark 13:26 NLT

Mark talks a lot about the return of Jesus in his gospel particularly in Mark Ch 13.

Jesus spoke about Noah's generation when He said,

"When the Son of Man returns, it will be like it was in Noah's day.
In those days before the flood, the people were enjoying banquets and parties and weddings right up to the time Noah entered his boat.
People didn't realize what was going to happen until the flood came and swept them all away. That is the way it will be when the Son of Man comes.
Matthew 24:37-39 NLT

When Jesus returns to reign it will be like it was in Noah's day.

The time that He returns is dependent upon the children of God.

Are we ready to receive the bride groom?

When will we learn to be the righteous bride who has adorned herself with white robes?

The groom is waiting for the bride to prepare herself.

If we are honest with ourselves we will recognise that we are far from that state whilst we live in religious divisions that segregate the body.

Whilst we appoint leaders who intervene on our behalf and who stand in the place of God's Spirit.

Whilst our members are convicted of abuses and money is paid for blessings that the Lord has given freely.

There is a need for much change to come about among us.

But we can be sure that He will return.

One way in which we are able to remove the divisions that we live with might be to dispense with the buildings that we meet in that support those divisions, and the weekly services that we attend that emphasise our differences, and instead meet with friends in varying locations and to go out of our way to create friendships with other Christians who we might not normally meet with, in different situations.

Do we want to demolish those strongholds of religious divide that the enemy has installed?

Are we, as Noah was, living in righteousness or do we cling to the security of the cliques that we are a part of?

The Lord had to wait until Methuselah and Lamech had died before He allowed righteous Noah aboard the ark to move into the new era.

Will we keep Him waiting for our death before the bride begins to prepare herself for the groom to come?

The purpose of Noah's ark was to bring salvation for anyone who wanted it.

Had the people of that time decided that they wanted to change, they could have had a ride into the new era but they didn't.

Just eight people travelled into the new era; righteous Noah, his wife, his sons and their wives.

Noah's ark is a picture for us to see what the Lord is doing at this time.

We too are moving into a new era, if we are sons and daughters of God and hearing what He is saying to us.

We are leaving behind the church era and moving into the era of God's kingdom.

The earth is being shaken and will continue to be shaken until all of God's chosen are safe.

Our eternal security will not be brought about by vaccine or climate change reversal or medical cures or social changes or world peace.

God has provided an ark.

It is in the process of being built.

Those who are wanting to move forward with the Lord are a part of the ark.

There is an invitation for anyone to become a part of that ark, to contribute to the establishing of God's kingdom on earth; to be secure.

In Noah's time, as today, the people around were busy building their own kingdoms.
They were not interested in building into God's kingdom.

The ark that God has provided is not a building or a system of rituals and dogma but is composed of a body of people who are built into living relationships.

Next we will move into the new era with Noah and look into the future.

Chapter 24.

Noah on the water

Genesis 8:1-14
But God remembered Noah and all the wild animals and livestock with him in the boat.

He sent a wind to blow across the earth, and the floodwaters began to recede.

The underground waters stopped flowing, and the torrential rains from the sky were stopped. So the floodwaters gradually receded from the earth.

After 150 days, exactly five months from the time the flood began, the boat came to rest on the mountains of Ararat.

Two and a half months later, as the waters continued to go down, other mountain peaks became visible. After another forty days, Noah opened the window he had made in the boat and released a raven.

The bird flew back and forth until the floodwaters on the earth had dried up.

He also released a dove to see if the water had receded and it could find dry ground. But the dove could find no place to land because the water still covered the ground.

So it returned to the boat, and Noah held out his hand and drew the dove back inside.

After waiting another seven days, Noah released the dove again.

This time the dove returned to him in the evening with a fresh olive leaf in its beak.

Then Noah knew that the floodwaters were almost gone. He waited another seven days and then released the dove again.

This time it did not come back. Noah was now 601 years old.

On the first day of the new year, ten and a half months after the flood began, the floodwaters had almost dried up from the earth.

Noah lifted back the covering of the boat and saw that the surface of the ground was drying. Two more months went by, and at last the earth was dry!

Noah is moving into a brand new era.

At the beginning of the book of Genesis we read that God's Spirit was *'hovering over the waters'. Genesis 1:2. NLT.*

The first era was beginning.

In scripture water often symbolises life or the entrance into new life.

In the arc, Noah and his family were heading into a new life - into a new era.

They can only travel into that place by travelling on the water in an ark.

In order to move into a new era, the Israelites also had to travel through water, the waters of the red sea.

To enter the land that had been promised they had to travel through the waters of the river Jordan.

Jesus too went through the waters of the river Jordan, at approximately the same place as the Israelites, when He was baptised by John.

It wasn't until Jesus had been through the waters of baptism that the Spirit alighted on Him and His ministry could commence.

Jesus told John that it was 'for the sake of righteousness' that He must be baptised.

But Jesus replied to him, "Permit it just now; for this is the fitting way for us to fulfill all righteousness." Then John permitted [it and baptized] Him.
Matthew 3:15 AMP

Jesus ushered in a new era of kingdom.

We too need to travel through the waters of baptism in order to enter the kingdom of God.

The Spirit is hovering over those waters at this time waiting for those who are willing to become one with Him.

Without becoming one with God's Spirit, water baptism is no more than a ritual carried out for the satisfaction of man and has no purpose for us in God's kingdom.

God is Spirit. If we are to become one with God, we too must take on God's Spirit in order to become a new creation.

We must recognise and invite God's Spirit in, He will not force Himself upon us. This is a first step of faith in our new life in God's kingdom.

Noah was called a man of righteousness because he heard and obeyed the Lord.

It was his faith, demonstrated by obedience, that enabled him to move, step by step, into the new era.

But God remembered Noah and all the wild animals and livestock with him in the boat.

The phrase, 'God remembered' doesn't give us permission to believe that God went off to do something else and completely forgot about Noah.

What it means is that God never forgot Noah. He was at the centre of God's purposes.

After one hundred and fifty days the flood waters began to recede and the ark rested on the top of mount Ararat which was situated in what is now Turkey.

It was two and a half months later that other peaks became visible and Noah waited another forty days before he sent a raven out to assess whether there was land that could sustain them.

Noah has been in the ark approximately two hundred and sixty five days.

A raven was sent out initially and it did not return to the ark but flew backwards and forwards.

The raven was sent out because Noah wanted to know if the land was habitable.

There was no way that Noah could see the land around as there was only an opening at the top of the ark.

The raven could live on dead carrion that floated on the water and so didn't need to return to the ark for food.

He then sent out a dove to find dry land but the dove returned as there was nowhere for it to rest or food for it to eat.

It's a good job that Noah has plenty of provision on board, he must be concerned that supplies are running low.

After seven days he released the dove again and it returned with an olive leaf and so Noah realised that things were beginning to grow again but there was still nowhere for the dove to rest and so it returned.

After another seven days he released the dove once more and the dove didn't return and so Noah realised that the earth was drying up.

Noah is now six hundred and one years old.

The text tells us that he has been in the arc ten and a half months.

Noah lifted off the covering that was on the ark and then waited another two months before he saw that the earth was drying up.

We often fail to notice that God is always in the background, in control, allowing His plans to unfold.

At the beginning of this chapter Moses tells us that the Lord sent a wind to blow across the land.

We can be sure that Noah and all on board appreciated that wind drying up the earth.

It was more than a year before God told Noah it was time to come out of the ark.

Those who have studied these things state that it was exactly one year and ten days.

The journey for Noah and his family wasn't an easy one.

He was safe, he had all he needed and he knew that he was living in the purposes of God but it must have been a very hard time.

We will look at what the new world has in store for them next.

Chapter 25.

Noah on dry land

Genesis 8:15-22. 9:1-17
Then God said to Noah, "Leave the boat, all of you—you and your wife, and your sons and their wives. Release all the animals—the birds, the livestock, and the small animals that scurry along the ground—so they can be fruitful and multiply throughout the earth."

So Noah, his wife, and his sons and their wives left the boat. And all of the large and small animals and birds came out of the boat, pair by pair. Then Noah built an altar to the Lord, and there he sacrificed as burnt offerings the animals and birds that had been approved for that purpose.

And the Lord was pleased with the aroma of the sacrifice and said to himself, "I will never again curse the ground because of the human race, even though everything they think or imagine is bent toward evil from childhood.

I will never again destroy all living things. As long as the earth remains, there will be planting and harvest, cold and heat, summer and winter, day and night."

Then God blessed Noah and his sons and told them, "Be fruitful and multiply.
Fill the earth.

All the animals of the earth, all the birds of the sky, all the small animals that scurry along the ground, and all the fish in the sea will look on you with fear and terror. I have placed them in your power.

I have given them to you for food, just as I have given you grain and vegetables.

But you must never eat any meat that still has the lifeblood in it. "And I will require the blood of anyone who takes another person's life.

If a wild animal kills a person, it must die. And anyone who murders a fellow human must die. If anyone takes a human life, that person's life will also be taken by human hands.

For God made human beings in his own image.

Now be fruitful and multiply, and repopulate the earth."

God told Noah and his sons, "I hereby confirm my covenant with you and your descendants, and with all the animals that were on the boat with you—the birds, the livestock, and all the wild animals—every living creature on earth. Yes, I am confirming my covenant with you.

Never again will floodwaters kill all living creatures; never again will a flood destroy the earth."

Then God said, "I am giving you a sign of my covenant with you and with all living creatures, for all generations to come.

I have placed my rainbow in the clouds.

It is the sign of my covenant with you and with all the earth.

When I send clouds over the earth, the rainbow will appear in the clouds, and I will remember my covenant with you and with all living creatures.

Never again will the floodwaters destroy all life.
When I see the rainbow in the clouds, I will remember the eternal covenant between God and every living creature on earth."

Then God said to Noah, "Yes, this rainbow is the sign of the covenant I am confirming with all the creatures on earth."

I am often bewildered as to why the bible has been split into chapters in the way that it has.

On many occasions the text has been randomly split apart whilst the author is continuing the story.

In other places the text is clearly beginning a new theme and yet has been included within a preceding story.

When reading scripture it is important to remember that the original text had no chapters or verses but was read as a whole and complete manuscript.

When we read about Noah and the story of the flood we often have pictures in our mind, images of the way that the story has been depicted in books, cartoons, jokes, on film and perhaps on television too.

We might imagine cartoon characters or brave movie stars. We tend not to think too seriously about the man of reality.

We can be sure that Noah would have had friends and relatives among the people who rejected his warnings.

His wife would have had family and so would the wives of his sons.

It must have been difficult for Noah to persevere with what he believed God was asking of him against the pressures that he must have faced.

We often forget, when reading about historical figures, that they were people who are similar to ourselves.

They had all of the emotions and feelings and trials that we experience.

Noah lived in a period before God had introduced any laws for men to live by and yet he was considered righteous.

Noah's righteousness wasn't dependent on keeping the law or by being good or even on his achievements, but on his obedience in carrying out what he had been asked to do.

There are many of us who have broken laws and have unpleasant characters, we live with failed marriages and other relationships, perhaps we have dabbled in seances, speaking to the dead, witchcraft and drug abuse or carried out acts of violence.

There are others who appear to live spotless lives, appear to be upright citizens, attend church services, hold a good employment record and perhaps do many good charitable works.

The truth is that whatever our lives look like, we are all in the same situation and the same condition.

Until we have come into God's kingdom and know Jesus, we live in the kingdom of satan and are subject to the law of sin and death.

We live in a condition of sin because we choose to ignore God. It is impossible to please God without faith, regardless of how we behave or speak.

Our standing with God is not dependent upon what we do and say, eat or not eat but on who we have faith in.

If we have faith in ourselves and our own abilities then we will never leave the kingdom of satan.

When we choose to have a faith that is based upon what Jesus has achieved on our behalf then we can move from the kingdom of darkness and death into God's kingdom of life.

Noah and his family have travelled into a new era. The Lord told them that they can come out from the security of the ark and enjoy the land that they have been given.

The Lord confirmed to Noah, his family and all of the birds and animals, including those *'small ones that scurry along the ground',* that He will never destroy mankind again, even though everything that they do, from the day they are born, is bent towards evil.

The Lord is only too aware that even, if and when, our intentions seem to be good, we have a judgement that is rooted in sin and therefore flawed.

We are incapable of making righteous judgements until we have our mind renewed and restored under the guidance of God's Spirit.

Whenever it rains God will place a bow in the sky as confirmation of His covenant with man and all that is living.

A bow, in scripture, speaks about God's protection.

There are many references to bows in the bible. Another one to note is in the book of revelation where the rider on a white horse carries a bow and wears a crown. *Rev. 6:2.*

The rider on the white horse appears to be Jesus and He carries a bow to symbolise His promise of protection as He wars against the enemy in order to free those who are enslaved.

Noah was quick to acknowledge the Lord when they came out of the ark.

The very first thing that he did, before looking for a good spot for a picnic or a place to stay for the night, was that he offered a sacrifice of thanks for their safe deliverance.

The Lord acknowledged where Noah's priorities lay by responding to Him.

Within the covenant that the Lord gave are the first words of guidance from the Lord that might be interpreted as law.

'Do not eat meat with the blood in it and if an animal or a human takes a life then that person or animal must die'.

The Lord gave Noah a reason for this, which is that, *'man is made in the image of God'.*

This is the second time that God has reminded us that we are not the same as the animals, birds or other creatures.

Our life comes from a different source.

The Lord gave Noah permission to eat meat with His blessing. This is a gift and permission that He has never taken back.

The main thrust of God's words to Noah and to the animals and birds is *to spread out, to be fruitful and to multiply.*

This too is a command that the Lord continues to leave with us today.

One of our purposes, when we are born into God's kingdom, is to reproduce others who will learn to take on the character of God, who is love.

We will leave Noah here to explore his surroundings. There is much for him to do.

Chapter 26.

Noah's sons.

Genesis 9:18-29.
The sons of Noah who came out of the boat with their father were Shem, Ham, and Japheth. (Ham is the father of Canaan.)

From these three sons of Noah came all the people who now populate the earth.

After the flood, Noah began to cultivate the ground, and he planted a vineyard.

One day he drank some wine he had made, and he became drunk and lay naked inside his tent. Ham, the father of Canaan, saw that his father was naked and went outside and told his brothers.

Then Shem and Japheth took a robe, held it over their shoulders, and backed into the tent to cover their father. As they did this, they looked the other way so they would not see him naked. When Noah woke up from his stupor, he learned what Ham, his youngest son, had done.

Then he cursed Canaan, the son of Ham: "May Canaan be cursed! May he be the lowest of servants to his relatives."

Then Noah said, "May the Lord, the God of Shem, be blessed, and may Canaan be his servant!
May God expand the territory of Japheth! May Japheth share the prosperity of Shem, and may Canaan be his servant."

Noah lived another 350 years after the great flood. He lived 950 years, and then he died.

It is significant that Moses, as he tells us who came out of the ark, explains that Ham is the father of Canaan.

Ham is the only son that he gives an explanation of in this way.

Moses was about to embark on a war against the Canaanites and so he wanted his readers to appreciate where the enemy had come from.

Although the three sons are usually listed in the order of Shem, Ham and Japheth, the eldest son was possibly Japheth according to alternative versions of the text, particularly the King James version and the amplified version (*Genesis 10:21*) and the youngest son was Ham. (*Genesis 9:24*).

Shem is always listed first in the bible as he is the father of the line that carried through to Abraham, from Moses' point of reference.

We know that line continued through to Jesus.

No doubt Noah was appreciating the fact that the ground was no longer cursed when he cultivated it and planted a vineyard.

I can't imagine that Noah's vineyard was the first thing that he set about to cultivate or that this was an event that happened very soon after they had left the ark.

Some time between leaving the ark and his death, some three hundred and fifty years later, Noah planted a vineyard and drank a little too much of its produce.

We assume that Ham just happened to be passing Noah's tent and accidentally saw him lying there naked, but the text indicates that Ham and his son Canaan were already in the tent with Noah.

Ham could have discretely covered his father, but instead, he went out and told his brothers about it.

The text implies that he was disrespectful of his father and was mocking him.

Japheth and Shem had a greater respect for Noah and didn't join in with his mockery but took a sheet and walked backwards so that they didn't see him to cover him up.

In the morning Noah discovered what had happened and cursed Ham's son.

I suspect that there is more to this story than we are given in Moses' writing.

Perhaps this was a well known story that everyone knew of and Moses didn't feel the need to expand on it more than telling of the bare bones.

Moses is simply telling us about the roots of the Canaanite nations, that they were founded in rebellion.

The fact is that it was Ham who was disrespectful at this time, we are not told of his other characteristics, this story tells us what we need to know about his character.

Ham's son may have been involved with this mockery of Noah but whether he was or not, he will, inevitably, inherit his fathers ways.

Canaan is the fruit of Ham.

Noah was a righteous man and his words carried the full force as if they had come from God.

Noah prophesied over his children and he says, *"May Canaan be cursed! May he be the lowest of servants to his relatives."*

Then Noah said, "May the Lord, the God of Shem, be blessed, and may Canaan be his servant!

May God expand the territory of Japheth! May Japheth share the prosperity of Shem, and may Canaan be his servant."

These aren't words spoken in anger by a man looking for revenge, but they are words of truth speaking about the inevitability of one thing leading to another.

The Lord laid out this same principle at the very beginning of creation when he fashioned all of creation to produce fruit after its own kind.

'Noah lived another 350 years after the great flood. He lived 950 years, and then he died'.

From the time of Noah's death we will discover that life expectancy will rapidly decrease.

Records from other cultures of that period tell us that Noah settled at the head of a large river.

I can imagine that river typifying the stream of civilisations that flowed from him.

We will continue to look at this flow of Noah's descendents in part two.

To contact Tim, the author - email:
warwickhouse@mail.com

Tim has also written:

Journey Into Life:

What did Jesus really preach about when He was on earth?
Within "A Journey into Life" we discover the joy of travelling to a new place.

Tim has set our search for God's kingdom in the form of a journey to a new land.

Once inside the new land we begin a journey of discovery – everything is new.

Did Jesus teach that His kingdom is within our grasp?
Is this a land – A kingdom that we can live in now – in our own lifetime?

The answer is yes!

Some Adjustments Required?:

We live our lives from day to day carrying out regular routines and rituals often without thinking about what we do and what we say and why.

We take for granted that the things that we have done and said and even for centuries past must be right because that is simply the way things are.

Tim has taken some of the many misunderstood concepts in the Christian life that we have for so long taken for granted and brought correction and redirection.

God is doing a new thing in this season and those who want to follow His direction need to hear Him.

A Time To Consider:

A Time to Consider was written at a time when several friends and friends of friends had been taken Ill by potentially life threatening illnesses.

When this happens to us out of the blue it is naturally a shocking discovery to realize that we aren't going to live on this earth, in this body, forever.

It is however a reality that we all need to take into consideration.

Any of us may be taken away at any time.
Our life on earth is a very short period when we consider eternity.

Let us get involved with eternity now - we may not get another opportunity to do so.

The Shaking:

We live in a changing era.
God is moving and the earth is being shaken.
The church age is passing.
God's kingdom age is upon us.
How do the times that we live fit with God's plan for us in eternity?
Has our own past affected our present and will it affect our future?
Can we make an impact in our time?

Our Foundations:

Many of us have missed out on vital foundational truths in our walk with the Lord.
Consequently we tend to wander around unaware that we may be missing out on the good things that Father has planned for us, unsure of where we should be or what our purpose is here on earth.
As we look into "Our Foundations" some much needed clarity and understanding will be gleaned for our benefit and for that of the emerging kingdom.

Genesis part one:

There are many apparent mysteries for us to uncover when reading the book of Genesis.
In Genesis part one we attempt to uncover and give an answer to some of these mysteries.
We also invite the reader to consider the text for themselves and to appreciate that the Lord is wanting us to open up a discussion with Him.

Genesis part two:

In Genesis part two we continue to look at the line of progression that began with Adam and will continue to the birth of Jesus.
Noah has journeyed into a new era. Life has continued as the Lord promised.
Abraham, the man of faith and the father of all who choose to trust in Jesus, is born.
The nations begin to emerge from the mists.

Genesis part three:

Genesis part three brings us to the birth of Isaac who is a type of Jesus.
From Isaac, through Jacob, to Joseph and into the land of Egypt we can journey with the patriarchs and the children of the man who becomes Israel.
The Lord is bringing His plan of redemption to pass.

EBooks by Tim Sweetman

Journey Into Life.
Some Adjustments Required?
A Time To Consider.
The Shaking.
Our Foundations.
Genesis part one.
Genesis part two.
Genesis part three.

Other recommended publications of related interest:

By John J Sweetman

Paperback and EBooks:

Establishing the kingdom series:

The Book of Joshua
The Book of Judges
The Book of Ruth
The Book of 1 Samuel
The Book of 2 Samuel
The Book of 1 Corinthians
The Book of 2 Corinthians
The Book of Galatians
The Book of Revelations
The Book of Romans
The Emerging kingdom
Babylon or Jerusalem – your choice

by Fiona Sweetman

Paperback and EBook
Taste the Colour Smell the Number

Printed in Great Britain
by Amazon